# Guide for Use of the Minimum Airfield Operating Surface Marking System

## U.S. Air Force

**AIR FORCE HANDBOOK 10-222, VOLUME 16**
**1 DECEMBER 2005**
*Certified Current 8 March 2012*

# GUIDE FOR USE OF THE MINIMUM AIRFIELD OPERATING SURFACE MARKING SYSTEM

**DEPARTMENT OF THE AIR FORCE**

This page left intentionally blank.

BY ORDER OF THE
SECRETARY OF THE AIR FORCE

AIR FORCE HANDBOOK 10-222, VOLUME 16

1 DECEMBER 2005

Certified Current, 8 March 2012

*Operations*

*GUIDE FOR USE OF THE
MINIMUM AIRFIELD OPERATING
SURFACE MARKING SYSTEM*

---

NOTICE: This publication is available digitally on the AFDPO WWW site at:
**http://www.e-publishing.af.mil.**

---

OPR: HQ AFCESA/CEXX
    (Lt Col Kent Nonaka)
Supersedes AFH 10-222, Volume 16,
    1 February 2001

Certified by: HQ AFCESA/CEX
(Colonel William E. Norton)
Pages: 77
Distribution: F

---

This handbook provides guidance for use of the Minimum Airfield Operating Surface Marking System (MAOSMS). It includes layout of the minimum operating surface and access routes necessary for emergency launch and recovery of aircraft, placement of markers, and use of the paint striping machine. The MAOSMS may be used to support immediate operations from a bomb-damaged runway or for initial bed down efforts to support a bare base deployment. The system identifies the usable runway surface in the shortest possible time in order to launch and recover combat aircraft. The expedient procedures in this handbook are emergency recovery actions performed when urgent mission requirements and insufficient time prevents restoring the markings to their original peacetime criteria.

Users of this handbook include the MAOSMS crewmembers – Engineering/ Structural Journeymen and augmenters required for layout, placement, and use of these systems. It is essential for the layout/marking and paint striping crew leaders to have a basic knowledge of the system, its operation, and maintenance requirements.

Guidance found in this handbook came from the references found in **Attachment 1**, which also contain additional information concerning management of airfield damage repair (ADR) operations:

This handbook provides guidance, but does not replace TO 35E2-6-1, *Minimum Airfield Operating Surface Marking System (MAOSMS)*. The TO takes precedence over this handbook in all cases. Personnel must have the applicable technical orders on site whenever performing minimum operating strip layout and marking procedures.

Use Engineering Technical Letter 04-7, *C-130 and C-17 Landing Zone (LZ) Dimensional, Marking, and Lighting Criteria* to mark landing zones used for aircrew training and contingency operations of C-130 and C-17 aircraft.

NOTE: Ensure all records created as a result of processes prescribed in this publication are maintained in accordance with Air Force Manual (AFMAN) 37-123, *Management of Records*, and disposed of in accordance with the Air Force Records Disposition Schedule (RDS) located at **https://webrims.amc.af.mil.**

*SUMMARY OF REVISIONS*

This change updates office symbols (throughout); updates the OPR and certified by lines (title page); updates governing directives for the program (page 71); added **Attachment 1**, *Glossary of References and Supporting Information*; added sand to the list of consumables in **Table 2.2.**; changes the format to comply with AFI 33-360, Volume 1, and other minor changes throughout.

# Chapter 1

# INTRODUCTION

**1.1.  Purpose.** The Minimum Airfield Operating Surface Marking System (MAOSMS) supports base recovery after attack operations as an expedient marking system to identify the minimum operating strip (MOS). Without appropriate airfield pavement marking in an exploded and unexploded ordinance laden environment, aircraft movement is hazardous and difficult. The MOS is the smallest acceptable length and width of an operating surface that will meet an aircraft's mission configuration for takeoff and/or landing, allow minimum clearances for operation, and be readied to meet mission required timeframes. The MOS may be larger than the minimum requirements for operations when there is little damage to the runway and most of the runway is recoverable. The MOS location is normally selected to allow *both launch and recovery* after minimal clearing of debris and safing, clearing, and removing unexploded ordnance (UXO). However, it may also be used for *immediate launch only* to support specific wartime or emergency mission circumstances.

**1.2. Capability.** The MAOSMS provides enough material and equipment to mark a MOS between 50 and 150 feet wide and between 5,000 and 10,000 feet long. In addition, the system can mark 25 to 50 feet wide taxiways. The MAOSMS is a visual marking system that provides:

1.2.1.  Markers and painting for the operating surface's threshold

1.2.2.  Painting for the centerline

1.2.3.  Markers for the edges

1.2.4.  Painting for taxiway access lines

1.2.5.  Markers for distance-to-go (DTG) identification

1.2.6.  Painting to eliminate existing airfield paint markings

1.2.7.  Markers for the mobile aircraft arresting system (MAAS)

**1.3.  Safety Summary.**

1.3.1.  Personnel responsible for determining correct and proper MAOSMS layout and marking procedures shall become thoroughly familiar with and frequently review the specific procedures and safety precautions listed in the technical order.

1.3.2.  Ensuring correct MAOS layout and marking is critical to the airbase recovery process. Incorrect minimum airfield operating surface (MAOS) striping or improper placement of edge, distance-to-go, and MAAS markers could result in major aircraft damage and potential loss of life to flight and ground personnel.

1.3.3.  Notify Airfield Operations of any system irregularities and/or of any obstructions on or near the runway.

**1.4.  General Information.** The MAOS consists of the MOS and access routes from aircraft staging locations. Staging locations may be hardened shelters, parking ramp revetments, or dispersed and camouflaged parking spots. Even under normal conditions, markings at an existing airfield may be hard to see on visual approach (**Figure 1.1.**). Debris, smoke, and haze from an attack worsen the situation by obliterating or obscuring markings and references. The MAOSMS allows pilots to visually acquire the airfield's operating surface on approach to a MOS (**Figure 1.2.**).

**Figure 1.1.  Contingency Airfield.**

**Figure 1.2.  Bomb Damaged Airfield with MAOSMS.**

# Chapter 2

# RESOURCES

**2.1. Personnel.** Two teams, totaling six individuals, perform the MAOS layout and marking.

2.1.1. Layout/Marker Placement: An Engineering Journeyman (3E551) and three assistants layout the MOS and access taxiways and then place the remaining elements of the MAOSMS.

2.1.2. Paint Striping: A Structural Journeyman (3E351) and one assistant use the paint striping set to mark the MOS and taxiways and black out confusing/unnecessary lines on the MOS and taxiways.

2.1.3. The Engineering Journeyman usually functions as the MAOSMS Crew Chief and must be qualified to layout the MOS, direct operations of the Layout/ Marking Crew, and coordinate efforts through the Airfield Damage Repair (ADR) Team Chief. The assistants should be trained on the basic layout requirements and be familiar with assembly of all markers. Team members should be physically capable of handling and positioning marker components.

2.1.4. The Structures Journeyman must be qualified to operate and maintain the paint striper equipment during painting and lay down of reflective beads. He, or she, must also understand the basic requirements for layout of the MOS, direct the efforts of the assistant, and coordinate efforts with the Layout/Marking Crew Leader and the ADR Team Chief. The assistant must be familiar with the basic operation of the equipment and capable of operating the vehicle among base recovery operations. The assistant should be physically capable of handling and loading heavy paint and glass bead supplies. *NOTE*: If the Paint Striper fails, manual application of paint with 2-gallon sprayers and rollers, and hand spreading of glass beads will be necessary, which will require additional manpower.

**2.2. System Equipment.** Four major equipment items associated with deployment of the system are: 1) A large flatbed or stake side truck to carry markers; 2) MAOSMS kit; 3) Paint Striping Set; 4) A pickup truck, with heavy-duty suspension and adequate loading/ towing capacity, used with the Paint Striper.

2.2.1. When deployed, a 2.5-ton cargo truck is suitable to carry the markers. If not available, use a truck with at least a 1.5-ton capacity or a flatbed trailer.

2.2.2. Two vehicles are required to efficiently and quickly layout and use the MAOSMS. If two vehicles are not available, use the truck to layout the cones and markers, and to pull the Paint Striper. If performing double duty, load most of the edge markers on flatbed trailers. This allows disconnection of the trailers after placing the markers. Not only will this prevent overloading the one available truck, but will also allow the truck to hustle between priorities without having marker frames and bases fall off the vehicle.

**2.3. System Components.** The components listed in **Table 2.1.** are part of the MAOSMS and should be in the kit. If there are missing components due to loss or damage, immediately reorder individual components per the parts listings in Technical Order (TO) 35E2-6-1 so they are on-hand upon arrival at the deployed location.

**2.4. Consumables.** In addition to the kit components, there are consumable items that must be available prior to attack and damage. **Table 2.2.** lists the consumables and the required on-hand levels. Order these items separately; they are not part of the MAOSMS deployment package. Order, or reorder, per the consumables listing in TO 35E2-6-1. Ensure all items are available upon arrival at the deployed location.

**Table 2.1. Major MAOSMS Kit Components.**

| Component Name | Quantity Provided |
|---|---|
| Edge Marker Base | 140 |
| Edge Marker Top | 152 |
| Mobile Aircraft Arresting System [Arresting Gear Marker (AGM)] | 4 |
| Distance-to-Go (DTG) Marker   (2 ea. of numbers 1 to 9) | 18 |
| Marker Crossbraced Bases and Upright Holders | 22 each |
| Paint Striping Set | 1 |
| 18-inch Traffic Cones [1] | 150 |
| 200-foot Measuring Tape [1] | 2 |
| Sand Bag [1] | 100 |
| D-Handle Shovel [1] | 2 |
| *NOTE:* [1] Required accessory items.  Ensure readily available during layout. | |

**Table 2.2. List of Consumables.**

| Component Name | Amount |
|---|---|
| Retro-reflective Beads (TT-B-1325, Type I [Gradation A] or Type III [Gradation A]) | 2,000 pounds [1] |
| White Traffic Paint—used for airfield marking (FS) TT-P-1952 | 200 gallons [1] [order 4 each 55-gallon drums] |
| Black Traffic Paint—used for obliteration of airfield/taxiway marking (FS) TT-P-1952 | 200 gallons [1] [order 4 each 55-gallon drums] |
| Yellow Traffic Paint—primarily used for taxiways (FS) TT-P-1952 | 100 gallons [1] [order 2 each 55-gallon drums] |
| White, Black, & Yellow spray marking paint | Twelve 20-oz cans of each color |
| Black & Yellow lumber crayons | 12 pack of each color |
| Paint Roller Frame and Handle | 6 each |
| Paint Roller Covers | 12 |
| Replacement Sandbags | 100 |
| *NOTE:* [1] Amounts listed are minimum requirements for a 150- by 10,000-foot MOS. | |

**2.5. Major Component Descriptions.** The MAOSMS includes a paint striping set and three types of markers: edge, DTG, and MAAS.

2.5.1. **Edge Markers.** An edge marker (**Figure 2.1.**) consists of a heavy, hard-rubber base and an inverted "V" shaped top; the base and top are joined together with hook-and-loop fasteners. The top is made of a polystyrene board and is faced with a reflective fluorescent orange colored cover. To prevent damage to aircraft, the top is frangible and easily replaceable. The base is 30 inches wide by 48 inches long and weighs approximately 50 pounds; the top legs of the "V" are 20 inches long and the spacing at the end of the legs is 20 inches. A 10,000-ft MOS requires 138 edge markers and 88 are required for a 5,000-ft MOS. Ten edge markers are placed on each side of, and in line with, the MOS threshold and departure end lines (**Figure 5.2.**). Place a single edge marker at 200-ft intervals along the sides of the entire length of the MOS. *NOTE.* Be aware that previously fielded cerise (i.e., cherry red) colored edge markers may be on site, such as those used for tactical airlift and special operations forces. If present and you require additional markers, use the cerise markers for edge and departure end threshold marking.

**Figure 2.1. Typical Edge Marker.**

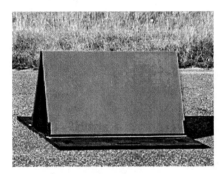

2.5.2. **Distance-to-Go (DTG) Markers.** A DTG marker (**Figure 2.2.**) is a free-standing, diamond shaped, bright orange, flexible plastic retroflective sign with a single-digit numeral on one side. Each edge of the diamond shaped sign is 48 inches long; the digits are 38 inches high and black in color. There is a 2-inch wide black border around the edge of the sign. They designate, in thousands of feet, the distance remaining to the end of the MOS. To prepare the sign for use, unfold and place on a vertical, crossbrace frame (see **Attachment 1** for pre-attack folding instructions). Mount the sign frame on a horizontal, folding crossbrace frame that has dual springs. The spring loaded frame allows the sign to deflect if hit by aircraft turbulence (see **Attachment 2** for assembly directions). Place signs so pilots can read the numbers in the direction of travel. For a bidirectional MOS, the sign on the left side will not present a visible number. Stabilize the markers by placing a minimum of one sandbag on each of two opposing legs. There are 18 DTG markers packaged in the system.

*NOTE:* In this section, and throughout this handbook, references to the left and right sides of the runway/MOS refer to the **PILOT'S LEFT and RIGHT** when facing in the direction of aircraft travel. **Attachment 3** provides a basic description of terms relating to a runway/MOS, which crewmembers need to be familiar with during layout and installation.

**Figure 2.2. Typical Distance-to-Go Marker.**

2.5.3. **MAAS Markers.** MAAS markers (**Figure 2.3.**), also referred to as arresting gear markers (AGMs), are similar to the DTG markers except that the 38-inch numeral is replaced with a 40-inch black, solid circle. The sign frame is the same as the DTG markers (see **Attachment 1** and **Attachment 2** for folding and assembly directions). Face markers so pilots can see their black circle on the right side of the MOS in the direction of travel. Place the signs at the arresting gear location so they are readable only on the right side. For a bidirectional MOS, the pilot sees the back of the left side sign, which will not present a visible solid circle. Stabilize in the same manner as the DTG markers.

**Figure 2.3. Typical Arresting Gear Marker.**

2.5.4. **MAOS Paint Striping Set.** The MAOS AF120SET Paint Striping Set (**Figure 2.4.**) is a palletized, trailer-mounted, mobile airless spray system with a trailing two-wheeled paint-gun carriage. The overall unit and trailer weigh 3,550 pounds empty and at least 5,450 pounds when loaded with paint and beads. The trailer is a 5- by 12-foot tandem axle trailer weighing 1,400 pounds. A truck with a pintle hook, located between 18- and 24-inches high, can tow the paint striping set. If the trailer is to be loaded with two drums of paint and solvent, the truck should have a towing capacity of at least 8,000 pounds. You may demount the main assembly from the trailer and load it into the bed of a 2-ton pickup truck. *NOTE:* When loaded into the bed of a pickup truck with a lower load capacity, the AF120SET unit may not be able to carry a full load of beads and paint.

**Table 2.3.  Paint Striping Set Specifications**

| *MAOS AF120SET Paint Striping Set Specifications* | |
|---|---|
| Power | 18 horsepower diesel engine that powers a hydraulic oil pump and a single stage air compressor.  The hydraulic pump is capable of operating at 2,000 PSI. |
| Paint Storage | Two 60-gallon paint tanks. |
| Bead storage | 500-pound capacity pressurized tank. |
| Paint Spray | 3-gun airless spray system.  Normally has a 0.035" orifice using a number 221-835 spray tip for wide lines; a number 221-435 spray tip may be used to provide taxi lines in lieu of manually adjusting the 221-835 spray tip. |
| Bead Spray | 3-gun pressurized spray system.  Normally has 11/32" diameter nozzle (number 45-106); can use smaller diameter nozzles (number 45-104 & 45-105) for various densities. |
| Control System | Skip-line unit capable of controlling each gun. |
| Hand Wand | A one-gun airless spray system.  The gun is mounted on a handle with two-wheel carriage, uses a 25-foot high-pressure hose, and operates at 500 to 800 PSI. |

**Figure 2.4.  MAOS Paint Striping Set.**

**Chapter 3**

**PLANNING FACTORS**

**3.1. The Situation.** When deployed, you may face wartime bomb, mortar, artillery, rocket, and/or missile airfield damage (**Figure 3.1.**). Damage may be craters, camouflets, and spalls. The minimum MOS is based on the width and length of a runway surface that will support the aircraft and mission configurations for emergency launch and recovery. The actual MOS may be larger and depends on numerous factors that will influence recovery, such as: 1) Timeframe for launch or recovery; 2) Physical damage to the runway operating surface; 3) Resources available to perform rapid runway repair; 4) Clearance requirements for UXO.

3.1.1. Emergency use of the MAOSMS is just that—emergency use. The mission and recovery situation at the deployment location largely dictates the markings used to identify the MAOS (**Figure 3.2.**). The markings provide acceptable wartime concessions to peacetime practices and standards in order to provide rapid launch and/or recovery.

3.1.2. The MAOSMS and Emergency Airfield Lighting System (EALS), can employ within acceptable mission planning timeframes for most useable launch and/or recovery surfaces. Depending on aircraft launch timetables, airfield marking can take place simultaneously with other airfield recovery tasks, or be one of the final actions completed because MAOS marking depends on several airfield and base recovery actions. MAOSMS and EALS layout and installation must mesh with:

3.1.2.1. Damage assessment

3.1.2.2. Rendering safe, clearing, and removing UXO along routes, MOS, and throughout the airfield

3.1.2.3. Large debris removal, initial sweeping, clearance of routes to the MOS, and at undamaged areas of the MOS

3.1.2.4. Airfield damage repair

3.1.2.5. Final debris removal, clearance, & sweeping on the MOS

3.1.2.6. Mobile aircraft arresting system installation

**Figure 3.1.  Bomb Damaged Airfield.**

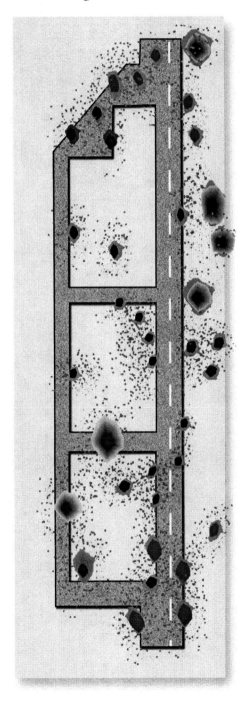

**Figure 3.2.  MAOS Selection on a Bomb Damaged Airfield.**

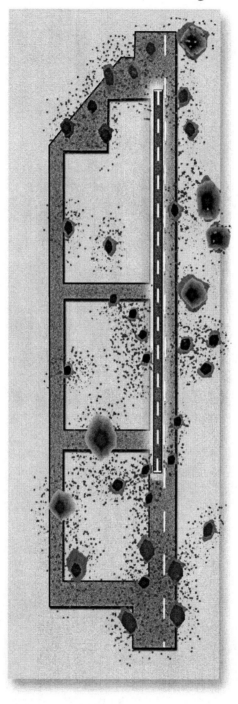

3.1.3. The TOs for the MAOSMS and EALS provide technical requirements for the operation and deployment of these systems. They provide a set of installation steps that will apply to almost all MOS layouts and provide a common reference point for system layout, planning, training, integrating the systems, and system checkout. However, be aware that the TOs may not provide an exact, final layout that is applicable for the installation of your MAOSMS and/or EALS.

3.1.3.1. The emergency at your location may require changes to the basic TO layout configuration. The MOS layout is acceptable and meets launch and/or recovery criteria when it meets the requirements of the Wing/Installation Commander.

3.1.3.2. If the Wing/Installation Commander's priority is for immediate launch, the initial MOS required only for launch of aircraft may not be the final MOS and may not include all expedient markings. In this scenario, the MOS will probably be unidirectional. The theater mission and Wing/Installation Commander's launch priorities can dictate one MOS for immediate launch purposes (even if not perfectly aligned to the runway's centerline), while preparations for a fully capable, larger, bidirectional MOS are under way for follow-on launch and recovery (See **Attachment 3** for handbook terminology).

**Example:** The Wing Commander at Bare Base X requires almost immediate launch of one fighter squadron after an air attack. The 150- by 10,000-ft runway is oriented in an 18/36 direction; the 36-end is the primary operational threshold. The runway is extensively damaged with large craters at both ends, and the ladder taxiways are also damaged. There are a large number of spalls and small UXOs. Providing a MOS for launch and recovery will take at least 6 hours. With limited UXO safing and sweeping, a 50- by 3,950-foot MOS for launching is available above the East-side damage. For this *launch-only* MOS, the Wing Commander only requires edge and DTG markers, and a MAAS installed 2,700 feet from the threshold. While launching, EOD will continue to safe and clear UXO. Other CE forces begin repairing the 36-end and a ladder taxiway for a 75- by 7,500-foot MOS. The final MOS requires complete MAOS marking, an EALS, and relocating the MAAS.

**3.2. Recovery Planning Factors.** Basic airfield recovery planning factors can vary. **Table 3.1.** lists basic factors that affect airfield recovery and layout of the MAOSMS. The table provides basic MOS (emergency) criteria; expected time-phased upgrades that may be required during recovery, and limitations to consider when working around conflicting airfield recovery tasks.

3.2.1. Close coordination with EOD personnel is necessary. As a minimum, EOD personnel must clear and safe the entire width of the MOS to include 100 feet beyond MOS edges and the first 1500 feet of MOS overrun. Rendering munitions safe will precede any marking activity by at least 2000 feet down the MOS surface prior to marking activities.

3.2.2. If the MOS is bidirectional, there are two operational thresholds. The one used most often is the primary operational threshold. For the purposes of this handbook, the threshold and departure ends for a unidirectional MOS are the same as the primary operational threshold and departure end for a bidirectional MOS.

**Table 3.1.  Basic Factors for ADR and MAOSMS Interaction.**

| ADR Event | Emergency Criteria | Limitations or Comments |
|---|---|---|
| UXO Identification & Safing at MOS | Assess, safe, & clear 100 feet on both sides of the MOS centerline, its overruns, & specifically identified areas. | Removal & clearing of some safed UXO may have to be limited to the MOS & work areas required for immediate launch.<br><br>Time phased upgrades are required:<br>- Assess, safe, & clear 100 ft from MOS edges, its overruns, & specifically identified areas.<br>- Assess, safe, & clear 100 ft off runway edges, its overruns, & at specifically identified areas. |
| Debris  Removal | Push debris at least 30 ft from edge of MOS & ensure debris is less than 3 ft high. | As time & mission allow, remove debris farther away from MOS & runway edges after areas are cleared of UXO.  Upgrades include:<br>- Removing debris at work areas for MAAS, EALS & its generators, & other airfield marking locations.<br>- Removing debris 75-ft from edge of MOS<br>- Removing obstructions that may block pilot's view |
| Threshold marking | Locate 10 markers on each side of threshold, starting 4 to 10 ft from edge of the MOS.<br><br>Paint an inverted "T" the full width of MOS at thresholds.  The "T" is a 30 to 36-inch wide solid white marking with retro reflective beads matching the centerline marking width. | Remove additional debris 40 ft from the ends of the MOS.  Ensure there are no obstructions blocking the pilot's view. |
| Centerline marking | Paint a white centerline stripe with retro reflective beads that is 30- to 36-inches wide by 50-ft long, separated by 50-ft long gaps. | |
| Table 3.1. continued on next page. | | |

| ADR Event | Emergency Criteria | Limitations or Comments |
|---|---|---|
| Distance-to-Go (DTG) Markers | Locate 25 ft from right side edge of MOS | If a conflict arises when the MAAS is installed up to 25 ft from the edge of the MOS:<br>- Install DTG markers 35-ft from edge of the MOS & at least 10-ft behind the MAAS.<br>- Remove debris near DTG markers that may block the pilot's view. |
| MAAS – Arresting Gear Marker (AGM) | Locate 35-ft from right side edge of MOS (in line with cable and behind the MAAS).<br><br>If coincident with a DTG marker, locate the AGM 5-ft outside the DTG marker. | Conflicts will arise for a narrow 50- to 60-ft wide MOS.  Even with the shorter barrier cable, the installed MAAS can extend into the 25- to 35-ft AGM placement area.  Installing the AGM at 35-ft would still be too close to the MAAS, obstructing the pilot's view.<br>- Install AGM on right side of the MOS, at least 10-ft from the MAAS.<br>- Clear any debris from around the MAAS and AGM that may block the pilot's view. |
| Edge Markers | Installed equal distance (between 4- & 10-ft) from each side of the MOS at 200-ft intervals | When the MOS is located along the edge of the runway, with few visual contrasts to delineate the edge of the runway from the shoulder, set the markers as close as possible to the edge of the MOS (i.e., 4-ft). |
| Table 3.1. continued on next page. | | |

| ADR Event | Emergency Criteria | Limitations or Comments |
|-----------|--------------------|-----------------------|
| Taxiway marking | With retro reflective beads, paint a 6-inch wide yellow stripe, starting 5 ft from the holding line that leads towards the MOS centerline with an arc having the maximum radius possible. Terminate on a line parallel and 3 ft from the MOS centerline. Use taxiway lines at MOS and around other curves near damaged sections of the taxiways and apron. | If there are straight sections of the taxiway not readily visible due to lack of contrast, paint a 6-inch centerline stripe through these areas. |
|  | Markers not typically employed. | If necessary and markers are available, place MAOSMS markers along taxiways when MOS supports emergency cargo airlift operations. - Place the markers between 10 and 15-ft away from the taxiway edge. Space markers up to 120-ft in turns and up to 220-ft in straight sections. - Increase the 10 to 15-ft distance if the aircraft's outboard engines overhang markers and/or the outboard engines are unable to operate at idle power while taxiing. |

*NOTE:* When time permits, black paint may be used to outline markings on light colored pavements. This makes them more prominent. Mark obstructions in contrasting colors to make them more conspicuous to pilots during daylight hours.

3.2.3. If installing an EALS system at the same time as, or in conjunction with the MAOSMS, accomplish EALS as part of the MAOSMS layout. In this case, additional layout requirements are necessary for the runway approach lighting, Precision Approach Path Indicator (PAPI) units, taxiway lighting, and EALS generators.

3.2.4. During initial MOS layout, set traffic cones at the correct positions for the approach lighting and PAPI units as a minimum. If additional UXO and debris clearing is required in order to complete the EALS installation along with the MAOSMS, check to ensure that the airfield base recovery timetable reflects integration of the MAOSMS and EALS.

3.2.5. **Table 3.2.** provides MAOSMS layout factors that provide a quick checklist of actions (and questions to ask) that will help to determine the system layout. The table is also applicable for planning rapid runway repair efforts along with MAOS marking. It provides information for the

MAOSMS Crew Chief to avoid conflicts during layout and installation of the MAOSMS and EALS. The Damage Control Center (DCC) and ADR Team Chief can use portions of this table to track information required for layout.

**Table 3.2.  MAOSMS Layout and MOS Planning Checklist.**

| Application | Required Action |
|---|---|
| __ 1.  MOS is required in lieu of full runway | __ 1) Are standard marking criteria required? |
| | __ 2) Will EALS: |
| | __ a)  Layout be accomplished with MAOSMS? |
| | __ b)  Be installed prior to placing markers? |
| __ 2.  MOS | __ 1) What is the width? |
| | __ 2) What is the length? |
| | __ 3) Is the MOS unidirectional or bidirectional? |
| | __ 4) Which end is the (primary) operational threshold? |
| __ 3.  MAAS | __ 1) Determine number of MAASs to install and installation location(s).  Determine cable length. |
| | __ 2) Determine MAAS set back distance from runway. |
| | __ 3) Determine if there are conflicts with other locations (DTG markers, edge markers & lights, PAPI units, etc.). |
| __ 4.  UXO | __ 1) If UXO are in the work area, obtain expected time to clear from runway and 100 feet from centerline. |
| | __ 2) If layout requires work at both ends of the MOS let the Survival Recovery Center (SRC) know that EOD may have to assess and safe both MOS threshold and departure ends to allow initial MOS layout. |
| | __ 3) Ensure that EOD is aware of which end of MOS will be the threshold (for early assessing & safing). |
| __ 5.  Threshold marking | __ 1) Will the inverted "T" and centerline be required initially if the initial MOS is for launch only? |
| | __ 2) Will the threshold markers be required initially if the initial MOS is for launch only? |
| | __ 3) Ensure "T" width matches centerline stripe width. |
| __ 6.  Centerline | __ 1) Based on MOS size, local conditions, available paint/bead supply, & set-up of Paint Striper, determine width of centerline stripe (i.e., 30 to 36 inches wide). |
| | __ 2) Are any crater repairs located within the MOS? |
| Table 3.2. continued on next page. | |

| Application | Required Action |
|---|---|
| __ 7. PAPI Light Location | __1) Check with the SRC to determine PAPI locations. Ensure location adjustments for differences in elevation between the PAPI, the runway reference point (RRP), and the RRP and the threshold elevations. [*NOTE*: the RRP is a point on the runway centerline adjacent to the PAPI units and is located where the visual glide path intersects the MOS.] |
|  | __2) If sited area has major variations in height, coordinate with ADR Team Chief to determine if leveling is possible.  Otherwise, SRC will adjust PAPI location. |
|  | __3) Are there any landing requirements or new obstructions that require a change in location or adjustment of the glide path approach angles? |
| __ 8.  Edge Markers | __1) Establish a standard edge marker setback distance from MOS edge between 4 and 10 ft. *NOTE*: Install edge lights 1 ft inside edge markers. |
|  | __2) Align initial edge markers at threshold to allow 10 markers on the left and right sides of the MOS. |
| __ 9.  Distance-to-Go (DTG) Markers | __1) Determine the available distance for DTG marker setback.  Consider UXO clearance, debris clearance, MOS width, & MAAS setback requirements. |
|  | __2) Check for conflicts with AGM. |
|  | __3) Determine spacing distances for MOS DTGs if uneven increments of 1,000 feet. |
| __ 10.  Arresting Gear Marker (AGM) | __1) Ensure UXO & debris is cleared to allow installation for MAAS setback. |
|  | __2) Determine required setback based on MAAS location, DTG markers, & unobstructed pilot's view of AGM. |
| Table 3.2. continued on next page. ||

| Application | Required Action |
|---|---|
| __ 11. Taxi line | __1) Obtain from SRC the minimum taxiway turning radius acceptable for mission aircraft. [*NOTE*: If specific data is not available, most fighter aircraft can use a 50-foot radius at low speed. Emergency shortfield operations of cargo aircraft (C-17 & C-130) can use a 90-ft radius.] |
| | __2) Determine beginning and end (i.e., lead-in and lead-out) locations for taxiway stripe arcs at the MOS. |
| | __3) Check for conflicts with edge clearance. |
| __ 12. Obliteration | __1) Determine if any airfield marking must be obliterated if MOS is for immediate launch. |
| | __2) Determine airfield markings to obliterate for normal MOS operations (i.e., launch and recovery). |
| __ 13. Reporting to ADR Team Chief/SRC | __1) Are there conflicts with (**Table 3.1.**) MAOSMS Emergency Installation Criteria? |
| | __2) Are there UXO & debris clearance problems, or set-back conflicts unresolved by ADR Team Chief/EOD? |
| | __3) Are there leveling problems or conflicts in siting the MAAS and PAPI? |
| | __4) Must marking criteria be changed to allow workarounds for the situation? |
| | __5) Contact SRC for obtaining the Wing/Installation Commander's approval of marking workarounds. |

**3.3. PAPI Location Planning Factors.** As listed in **Table 3.2.**, adjust standard PAPI location (950-feet from the end of the threshold) if there is: 1) a large enough difference in the height of the PAPI units from the runway reference point (RRP) for approach alignment; 2) An approach obstruction; and/or 3) a runway slope from the threshold to the RRP.

3.3.1. For MOS use under emergency conditions, units should be within 1-foot of the RRP elevation to use the standard 950-foot distance. Beam centers of both units **must be** within 1-inch of a horizontal plane; the horizontal plane shall be within 1-foot of runway elevation at the RRP.

3.3.2. On existing airfields, approach obstructions will not normally affect the glide path approach angle for the PAPI units. Most airfield locations were sited to meet obstruction criteria. Placing a MOS inside the existing runway surface will also avoid obstructions unless an attack has created new obstacles from displaced debris.

3.3.3. The normal setup is to place PAPI cone markers 950-foot from the threshold. It is very important, especially for emergency recovery of aircraft, to provide enough stopping distance on a short MOS. Adequate stopping distances are affected by the weather and pavement condition, especially in wet conditions and there is no porous friction course. **For short MOS operations where stopping** distance is a major consideration, there are four approaches to PAPI placement and installation that will provide increased MOS lengths for safer braking distances.

3.3.3.1. The first approach is to use the **exact PAPI to threshold distance** if that distance is less than 950 feet. **Figure 3.3.** provides a graphic range of values for installing the PAPI from the threshold based on the PAPI installation formula found in AFH 10-222 Volume 7, *Emergency Airfield Lighting System (EALS)*. The formula provides the exact PAPI placement from the threshold when PAPI units are level with, or up to 10 feet lower than, the MOS centerline adjacent to the PAPI. It provides distances from the threshold to the PAPI location based on glide slope angles ranging from 2.5 to 4.0 degrees, and height variations between 0 and 10 feet. The figure applies to fighter aircraft and cargo aircraft that are capable of, and approved for, short field landings. As indicated in **Figure 3.3.**, fighter aircraft can normally land with a PAPI distance to threshold less than the standard 950-foot distance. This is true even with large differences in elevation between the PAPI and the MOS. However, if the PAPI is adjusted for a 2.5 degree glide path approach angle for fighter aircraft, the 950-foot distance must be increased for height differences more than 2 feet.

**Figure 3.3. PAPI Distances from the Threshold.**

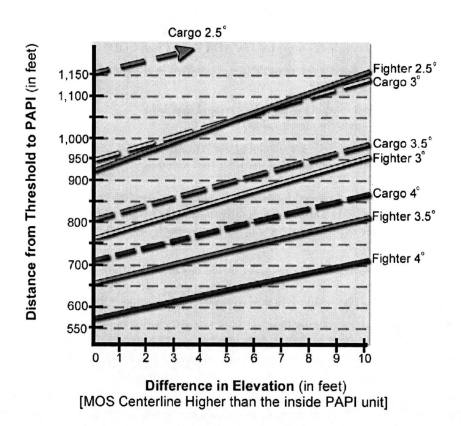

3.3.3.2. A second approach is to raise the **PAPI mounting height** to the same level as the MOS centerline. This will eliminate the need to increase the distance from the threshold or to change the standard 3.0 degree angle of the PAPI units. The Layout/Marking Crew Leader must identify the proper increase of PAPI elevation.

3.3.3.3. A third approach is to increase the **glide path approach angle** above 3.0 degrees in order to provide additional runout area for stopping. This method is only feasible for fighter aircraft and cargo aircraft that are capable of, and approved for, short field landings.

3.3.3.4. The fourth approach is to use a **combination** of the methods above to increase the MOS length for safe braking distances.

3.3.4. There may be numerous additional reasons requiring PAPI relocation other than braking concerns, such as conflicting with the required MAAS location, the initial PAPI location is too close to the taxiway, major damage, smoke and damage at the runway or approach zones, or other obstructions.

3.3.5. The Survival Recovery Center (SRC) and DCC should consider all of the above siting the overall MAOS. If a conflict becomes evident when siting the PAPI and/or MAAS, contact the ADR Team Chief and the DCC/SRC to consider relocating the units based on the above approaches. Only the SRC can approve the relocation and adjustment of the PAPI units. Also, contact the ADR Team Chief to address leveling the PAPI unit locations if necessary.

3.3.6. Even when there are no extreme variations in height along the runway and MOS, you may have to consider leveling the area where the PAPI units are located if there is a variation in elevation of more than 1 foot between the inside PAPI unit (beam center) and the MOS centerline. In this case, consider grading the areas between the MOS and the PAPI units to bring the units closer to the elevation of the MOS centerline. This will provide a flatter reference plane for pilots and helps eliminate disorientation.

3.3.7. An **important** point to keep in mind is that the PAPI units within the EALS are a two-box L-881 system. They are less precise than the standard four-box L-880 PAPI system. Position the centerline of the inside unit 50 to 60-feet from the edge of the runway. Position the outside unit 20 to 30 feet (see AC 150/5345-28D, par. 21.b.) from the inside unit. **This separation is the distance between the outside edge of the inside PAPI unit and the inside edge of the outside PAPI unit.** The larger separation increases the useable range of the system.

3.3.8. Some airfields that slope up or down from the threshold may already have established peacetime adjustments for the threshold and glide path approach slope. If so, these peacetime adjustments for approach lighting should be considered for use with the MOS if the MOS falls within the same runway elevation slopes. For more details on adjusting PAPI locations, based on runway to threshold slopes, see AFH 10-222, Volume 7, *Emergency Airfield Lighting System (EALS)*.

## Chapter 4

## BASIC CONFIGURATION LAYOUT

**4.1. Initial Marking.** Initial efforts are concentrated on the basic configuration layout of the MOS and access taxiway(s) by placing the MAOSMS traffic cones, or other expedient marking devices, such as marking paint or lumber crayons (Keel). The initial marking is to establish the key points for: the MOS and taxiway(s), installation of MOS and taxiway markers, painting, and location of the PAPI and approach lights. The first priority is to establish the location for the MOS centerline and the operational thresholds.

4.1.1. Based on current threats, a MOS supporting both launch and recovery can be located such that it is parallel to the runway centerline. This will allow the runway centerline to be used as the reference point for establishing the MOS centerline. The MOS boundaries become an important reference for all ADR work within and around the edge of the MOS. If the runway does not have an established pavement reference marking system (PRMS), consider installing one as a pre-attack effort to expedite MAOSMS installation and use.

4.1.2. A PRMS should have a zero point established for each pavement feature (i.e., runway, taxiway). The runway threshold at one end becomes the zero point. Paint marking on the pavement edges is set up at regular 50- and 100-foot intervals. Raised vertical markers are placed every 100 feet and are located away from the edges of the runway. Do not locate the raised markers too close to the edge of the runway, as the markers could interfere with recovery efforts and the deployment of the MAOSMS and EALS. A distance of 75 to 100 feet from the edge of the runway should be sufficient for most threats.

**4.2. Basic Layout. Table 4.1.** provides a quick checklist of procedures for configuring the basic layout. You may use it as a familiarization guide when installing the MOS. The DCC, MAOSMS, and ADR Team Chiefs can also use it to track progress of the MAOSMS efforts. **Figure 4.1.** depicts layout requirements for a unidirectional MOS with a taxiway at the operational and departure ends of the MOS, and identifies key reference points as described in **Table 4.1.** NOTE: If this was a bidirectional MOS, a second set of approach lights would be required at the other end and the access taxiway layout would change in **Figure 4.1.** to accommodate the approach lights.

**4.3. Taxiway Paint Striping Layout.** The Marking/Layout Crew establishes locations for all taxiway intersections with the MOS and for taxiway stripes that have changes in direction around damaged sections of a taxiway. The Paint Striping Crew normally performs the detailed layout for taxi line striping. The following information is provided for the Paint Striping Crew.

4.3.1. **Figure 4.2.** depicts typical taxi line stripe layouts. The 6-inch stripe begins 3-ft to the near side of the MOS centerline and extends to a point 5-ft from the taxiway holding line. The curved portion should have a smooth, constant radius arc that starts on the MOS. The arc:

4.3.1.1. Should be a constant radius curve with max arc possible

4.3.1.2. Must be at least as large as the **minimum taxi turning radius ($R_m$)** for the operational aircraft in its mission configuration

4.3.1.3. Must ensure that the **minimum taxiway width** (provided by the SRC) can be maintained without running off the edge of the full strength pavement or repaired surface

4.3.1.4. Must have a **min. radius** at least half the min. taxiway width

4.3.1.5. Should end prior to the taxiway holding line

4.3.2. Extend the start end of the curve (on the MOS) for a distance of 200 feet parallel to the MOS centerline. Based on the radii of the taxiway arcs, the Paint Striping Crew may use the Hand Wand to paint the taxiway stripe or use the Paint Striper. If the radius of a turn is too tight for the Paint Striper, the crew may use marker paint or Keel when laying out the curve. The Paint Striping Crew will mark the:

4.3.2.1. Exact locations for the start and end of the arc(s).

4.3.2.2. Intermediate points on the arc.

4.3.2.3. 200-foot lead-in line.

4.3.2.4. Centerline stripe from the arc to 5-ft short of holding line.

**Figure 4.1.  Example of Unidirectional Configuration Layout.**

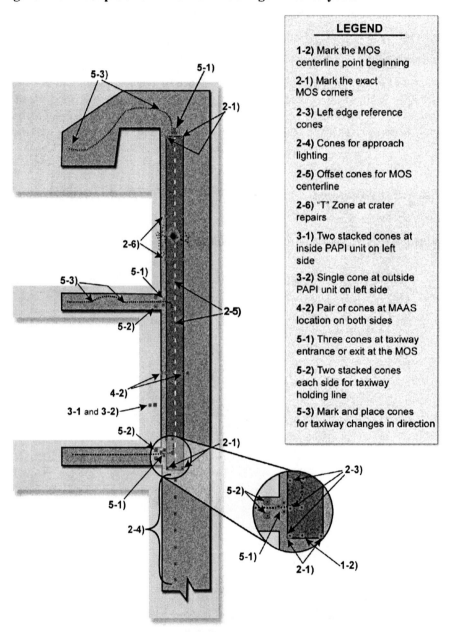

**LEGEND**

**1-2)** Mark the MOS centerline point beginning

**2-1)** Mark the exact MOS corners

**2-3)** Left edge reference cones

**2-4)** Cones for approach lighting

**2-5)** Offset cones for MOS centerline

**2-6)** "T" Zone at crater repairs

**3-1)** Two stacked cones at inside PAPI unit on left side

**3-2)** Single cone at outside PAPI unit on left side

**4-2)** Pair of cones at MAAS location on both sides

**5-1)** Three cones at taxiway entrance or exit at the MOS

**5-2)** Two stacked cones each side for taxiway holding line

**5-3)** Mark and place cones for taxiway changes in direction

**Table 4.1. Basic Configuration Layout Checklist.**

| Procedure | Actions |
|---|---|
| ___ 1. Establish MOS frame of reference | ___1) Using runway centerline & distances from runway reference system (if available), locate beginning of MOS centerline point. [A temporary immediate-launch-only MOS may not be exactly parallel to runway centerline, so determine centerline end-point and departure end corners] |
| | ___2) Mark exact beginning of the MOS centerline point. |
| ___ 2. Layout Centerline | ___1) Place cones on exact points of MOS corners |
| | ___2) Accomplish initial centerline three-cone alignment |
| | ___3) Place three-cone alignment on left edge of MOS |
| | ___4) Layout and place cones for approach lighting |
| | ___5) Layout the MOS centerline |
| | ___6) Mark crater repair areas with a T-zone (**Figure 5.1.**) |
| ___ 3. PAPI Location | ___1) Site the inside PAPI unit using two stacked cones 50 feet from the left edge of the MOS. |
| | ___2) Site the outside PAPI unit by placing a single cone 20 feet outboard and in line with the stacked cones. |
| ___ 4. MAAS Location | ___1) Determine MAAS location with SRC coordinates |
| | ___2) At MAAS location, place a cone on both edges of MOS and another cone 3 feet outboard of first cones. |
| ___ 5. Taxiway Location | ___1) Mark taxiway access with 3 cones placed in a triangle at intersection of taxiway centerline and MOS edge. |
| | ___2) Mark holding position lines with two stacked cones on both edges of taxiway, 100 feet from MOS edge. |
| | ___3) Mark out & place cones for access taxiway direction changes by placing at least 5 cones in each turn. |

4.3.3. If the Hand Wand is used, offset the cones about 9 inches to the left of the exact position. If the Paint Striper can be used for painting the stripes, then offset the marks or cones to the left based on the offset distance required for the gun. This offset distance can be adjusted based on:

4.3.3.1. Radius of the arc

4.3.3.2. Setup of the Paint Striper

4.3.3.3. Setup of the tow vehicle

4.3.3.4. Setup of vehicle carrying the (demounted) paint striping unit

**Figure 4.2.  Typical Layouts for Taxiway Lead-in/Lead-out Stripe.**

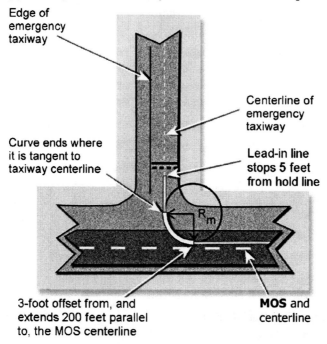

Edge of
emergency
taxiway

Centerline of
emergency
taxiway

Curve ends where
it is tangent to
taxiway centerline

Lead-in line
stops 5 feet
from hold line

$R_m$

3-foot offset from, and
extends 200 feet parallel
to, the MOS centerline

**MOS** and
centerline

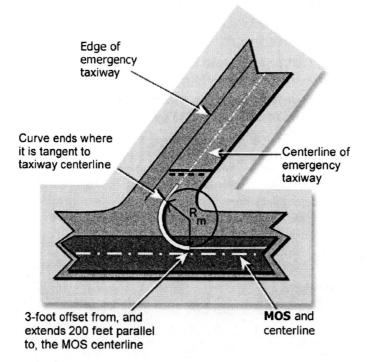

Edge of
emergency
taxiway

Curve ends where
it is tangent to
taxiway centerline

Centerline of
emergency
taxiway

$R_m$

3-foot offset from, and
extends 200 feet parallel
to, the MOS centerline

**MOS** and
centerline

4.3.4.  In some cases, an acute angle, high-speed emergency taxiway may be used. A MOS with an acute angle taxiway is shown in the bottom portion of **Figure 4.2.** You must provide at least the minimum taxi turning radius at the entrance of the taxiway that requires the reversing-type turn. The taxi turning radius for an aircraft traveling in the opposite direction will be longer in order to provide a smooth arc that intersects at the same position on the taxiway (**Figure 4.3.**) as the minimum taxi turning arc. When laying out the arcs, the distance CB is normally about equal to distance AB, as shown in **Figure 4.4.** CB and AB are the distances from the two points at the start of the curve on the MOS offset (Points C and A) to a point at the imaginary intersection of the emergency taxiway centerline with the MOS centerline offset (Point B).

4.3.5.  During emergency use, set up of a long taxiway curve that meets design standards is unlikely. When the acute angle is less than 45 degrees, the radius necessary to create a smooth curve ($R_{smooth}$) that meets peacetime taxiway criteria would create an arc too long for the MOS.

> **Example:** To meet peacetime (FAA) criteria, a 30-degree taxiway entrance would have a radius ($R_{smooth}$) of 800 feet and the distance CB would be more than 700 feet. It is not possible to quickly lay out a radius curve this large under emergency conditions, especially when UXO are present.

4.3.6.  For CB distances that are excessive, or would cause the aircraft to stray beyond the edge of the full strength pavement (**Figure 4.5.**), use Point B as the basis for design. For the two centerlines meeting at Point B, cut an arc tangent to the two centerlines using a radius equal to $R_m$.

4.3.7.  There are circumstances that may dictate different curve types such as when a crater obstructs the lead-on area to the taxiway or where severely acute angles make Point B too great a distance to fit the MAOS. In this case, adjoining curves could be necessary. Determine a point on the minimum radius arc where a 45- to 90-degree turn (**Figure 4.6.**) would hit the arc. Start the tangent to the curve at that point using a radius equal to or greater than $R_m$. As with all workarounds, clear them through the ADR Team Chief, DCC, SRC, and Wing Operations Center.

**Figure 4.3. Typical Taxiway Stripes for an Acute Angle Taxiway.**

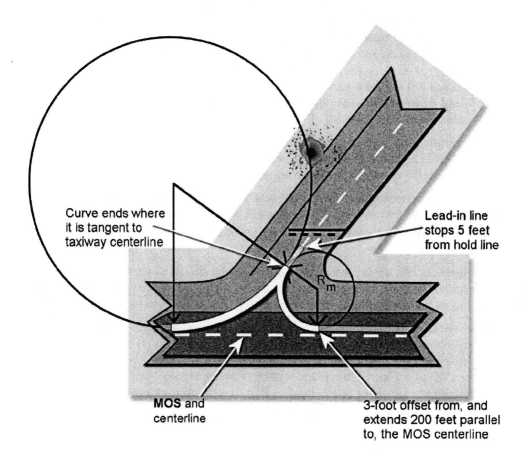

Curve ends where it is tangent to taxiway centerline

Lead-in line stops 5 feet from hold line

**MOS** and centerline

3-foot offset from, and extends 200 feet parallel to, the MOS centerline

**Figure 4.4.  Typical Layout Measures for an Acute Angle Taxiway.**

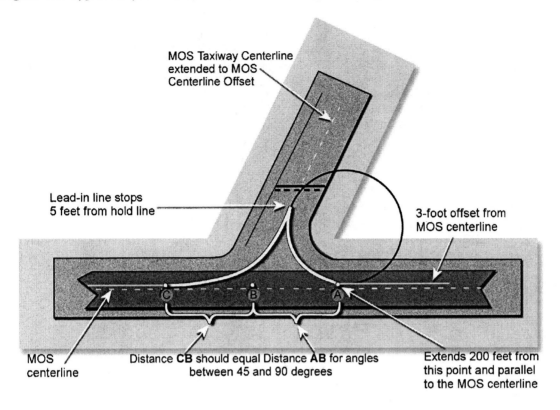

**Figure 4.5. Workaround Layouts for Excessive Length Arc.**

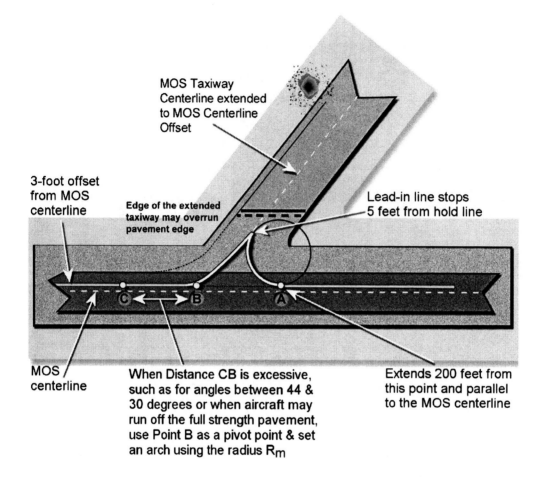

MOS Taxiway
Centerline extended
to MOS Centerline
Offset

3-foot offset
from MOS
centerline

**Edge of the extended
taxiway may overrun
pavement edge**

Lead-in line stops
5 feet from hold line

MOS
centerline

When Distance CB is excessive,
such as for angles between 44 &
30 degrees or when aircraft may
run off the full strength pavement,
use Point B as a pivot point & set
an arch using the radius $R_m$

Extends 200 feet from
this point and parallel
to the MOS centerline

**Figure 4.6. Workaround Taxiway Layout at Restricted Locations.**

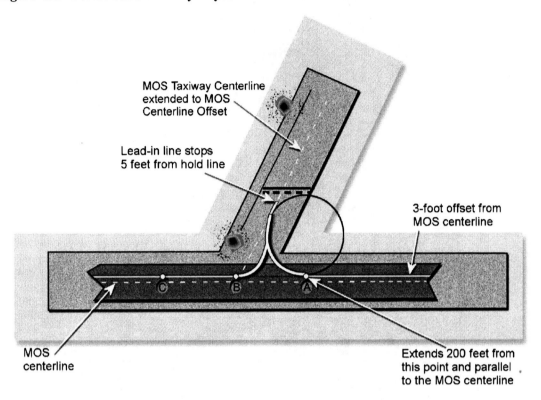

MOS Taxiway Centerline
extended to MOS
Centerline Offset

Lead-in line stops
5 feet from hold line

3-foot offset from
MOS centerline

MOS
centerline

Extends 200 feet from
this point and parallel
to the MOS centerline

**4.4. Layout for Taxiway Changes in Direction.** The Layout/Marking Crew lays out the taxiway center-line for changes of direction to avoid unrepaired craters or spall fields. The Layout/Marking Crew places cones at changes of direction around the damage. There is one cone each at the beginning and end of a curved section. Ideally, three evenly spaced cones are placed between the beginning and end cones, but this can vary based on length of the curve and radius of the curve. The recommended practice is to use 5 cones per curve and separate each change in direction of the curve by 25 feet. For some situations this may not be possible, such as when the area is restricted to a short length. If the length of the offset is short, but the offset distance around the damaged area allows it, make changes of direction more or less contin-uous when laid out with smooth transition large radius arcs. One cone may have to mark the coinciding beginning and end points for two curved sections. **Figure 4.7.** depicts a situation for laying out a taxiway centerline stripe around a damaged section of taxiway. It shows one section where 25-foot spacing can be used between curves, but also shows a modified section with smooth transition, short offset curves. To provide proper alignment for the Paint Striper or Hand Wand, offset the cones to the left of the exact taxi-way stripe (in the paint striper direction of travel). Determine required offset with the Paint Striping Crew. As with many tight arcs, the Paint Striping Crew will normally use the Hand Wand for the arc sections. When unable to coordinate ahead of time, mark the exact centerline for the points of the curve directly on the pavement by using marker paint or Keel. The Paint Striping Crew can choose the method for painting and offset cones as required.

**Figure 4.7.  Cone Layout Around Taxiway Damage.**

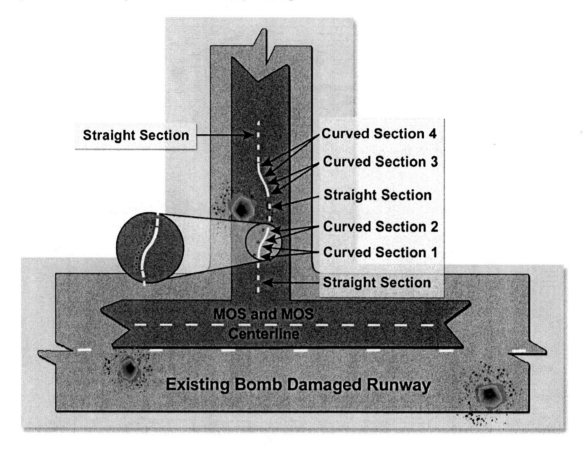

## Chapter 5

## INSTALLATION

**5.1. Instructions for MAOSMS Use.** The following tables provide detailed instructions for use of the MAOSMS. **Table 5.1.** is a general-purpose pre-attack checklist. The post-attack procedures in **Table 5.2.**, **Table 5.3.**, and **Table 5.3.** should be followed after completing the checklist in **Table 3.1.** Post-attack procedures for the Layout/Marking Crew are in **Table 5.2.** and **Table 5.3.** Post attack procedures for the Paint Striping Crew are in **Table 5.5.** When an asterisk (*) follows a major heading or step in the table, there is additional specific information provided for that heading/step following the table.

**5.2. Pre-Attack Efforts.** Perform the actions in **Table 5.1.** when in a high threat area to be prepared in case hostilities breakout.

**Table 5.1. General Purpose Pre-Attack Checklist.**

| Procedure | Actions |
|---|---|
| __ 1. Vehicles | __1) Identify and locate the following from Supply, Transportation, and CE resources:<br>   __ a) Two vehicles or a vehicle and utility trailer,<br>   __ b) Paint striping equipment,<br>   __ c) Paint supplies and glass beads<br>   __ d) Edge markers and vertical sign type markers. |
| __ 2. Pre-positioning equipment & supplies | __1) With EALS team, identify several possible locations (at both ends & middle of runway) for locating the EALS generator to support a 5K-ft MOS.<br>__2) Identify with DCC dispersal equipment locations.<br>__3) Pull & preposition supplies/equipment (see **Table 2.1. & Table 2.2.**; order supplies to meet minimum quantities:<br>   __ a) Traffic cones (5K-ft MOS: 68 ea; 10K-ft: 93 ea).<br>   __ b) Edge & threshold markers (5K-ft MOS: 88 ea; 10K-ft: 138 ea).<br>   __ c) Folding upright marker stands & base units (from 5 ea for a 5K-ft unidirectional MOS with 1 MAAS, up to 22 ea for a 10K-ft bidirectional MOS w/2 MAAS).<br>   __ d) Obtain and fill sandbags (44 minimum for a bidirectional 10K-ft MOS). |
| __ 3. Ready upright markers | ___1) At the prepositioning location, unpack the AGM and DTG markers from their storage bags.<br>___2) Attach sign faces to cross braces (see **Attachment 1**) |
| Table 5.1. continued on next page. | |

| Procedure | Actions |
|---|---|
| ___ 4.  Ready/Load edge markers | ___1) At pre-positioning location(s), remove appropriate amount of edge markers from their storage containers **(SRC should pre-designate the minimum MOS size for planning purposes)**.  Leave remaining markers in storage and save materials for repacking. <br> ___2) Load marker bases and "V" tops onto the truck or utility (flatbed) trailer. <br>     ___ a)  Bases & V-tops should be stacked separately & not preassembled.  Secure the V-tops to prevent them blowing off vehicles during transport. <br>     ___ b)  Arrange stacks for easy offloading.  Offload over sides or end of vehicle, whichever is quicker. |
| ___ 5.  Ready paint & bead supplies | ___1) Determine basic quantities of paint & beads required for pre-designated MOS size. <br> ___2) Preposition the paint & beads as necessary based on expected MOS size and usage. <br> ___3) Thoroughly mix paint with agitator included with the AF120SET paint striper. <br>     ___ a)  Alternative: Lay paint drums on sides; roll them to mix and agitate paint. <br>     ___ b)  Avoid puncturing or denting the drums while handling and mixing. <br><br> **CAUTION** <br> Paint drums are very heavy; use care when handling drums. |
| ___ 6.  Ready Paint Striper | ___1) Service/prepare paint striper per TO 36C35-7-1. <br> ___2) Install appropriate paint and bead tips.  Calibrate for 6- to 8-mil wet film thickness.  Actual thickness may vary based on paint viscosity, surface temp/moisture, air temperature, etc. * |
| Table 5.1. continued on next page. | |

| Procedure | Actions |
|---|---|
| | ___3) Ensure skip-controller is calibrated for 100-feet and set for a 100-foot cycle and 50-foot paint IAW TO 36C35-7-1. |
| | ___4) Calibrate bead delay timer. |
| | ___5) Obtain or mix the cleaning solution/solvent. Flush system as required for paint types and check the system. |
| | ___6) Determine offset for painting the centerlines. Notify the Layout Crew if unable to use the normal 2-foot cone offset, or exact centerline mark points.  * |

* *Notes* for Table 5.1.

**Step 6.2):** Various tips are available for the Paint Striper. If a 6-inch wide taxi stripe is to be painted, a tip that paints a 6-inch wide line may be used in place of the standard tip that provides a 12-inch wide line. However, the standard 12-inch tip can be used in many cases to provide the 6-inch wide line by angling the spray tip, cutting back on the paint spray density, and/or lowering the nozzle. Consider these factors when setting up the paint guns: the paint; the air; the paint and surface temperatures; moisture levels; and paint viscosity.

**Step 6.6):** The normal cone offset for the Paint Striper is 2-feet left of the centerline when using standard utility vehicles. However, when you are deployed, the only vehicles available at the contingency location may not be standard utility vehicles. In this case, the bumpers, visual sight lines over/around the fenders, truck cab height, and truck bed height/width could affect the required offset distance, especially if the Paint Striping unit is demounted from the trailer and placed in the truck bed. If the aiming pointer and paint-gun carriage can not be adjusted to accommodate the normal 2-foot offset, the Paint Striping Crew Leader must inform the Layout Crew Leader to use a different centerline cone offset. If cones are not available, the Layout Crew will mark the exact centerline directly on the pavement. If the vehicle and Paint Striper is incapable of operating directly over the centerline (i.e., without an offset), advise the Layout Crew Leader of the required offset.

## 5.3. Post-Attack Procedures for Layout/Marking Crew.

5.3.1. Perform the **layout** procedures in **Table 5.2.** after an attack, or when establishing a bare base airfield with poor/no markings.

**Table 5.2.  Marking Crew Post-Attack Cone Layout Procedures.**

| Procedure | Actions |
|---|---|
| __ 1. Vehicle Checkout and Employment | __1) Ensure vehicles and trailer(s) are still operable.<br>__2) Based on runway damage and choice of MOS, determine if distribution of marking resources on vehicle(s) and trailer(s) will need to be adjusted.<br>__3) Select best routes & crewmember use for layout. |
| __ 2. Threshold | __1) Based on the MOS identifier provided by the SRC/DCC, locate the MOS position on the runway.<br>__2) Determine exact centerline and threshold corners.<br>__3) Mark the pavement at each location and place a cone on each mark.  *NOTE*: The centerline and two threshold cones create a T-pattern with the centerline.  *<br>  __ a) When cones are available, offset MOS centerline cones 2-feet left of exact centerline (to create an offset centerline for aligning the paint striper).  *<br>  __ b) If paint marking is being used in lieu of traffic cones, do not offset the centerline.<br>  __ c) Measure down centerline 400 feet & mark pavement at exact MOS centerline.  Place a cone 2-feet left of mark.<br>  __ d) A person sights along the two offset cones at threshold centerline cone while directing placement of cone at the 200-foot point.<br>__4) Look towards approach zone from threshold centerline. Estimate if 1,400 feet of clear zone area is available for approach zone lighting.  Notify ADR Team Chief if approach zone area requires debris clearing. |
| __ 3. Centerline | __1) Mark MOS centerline.  Establish a distance control method to ensure accurate 200-foot spacing.  *<br>  __ a) Place cones at 200-foot intervals along the 2-foot offset centerline.  [Offset may have to be adjusted by Paint Striping Crew.]  Cones are called "centerline cones."  *<br>  __ b) If using paint markings in lieu of cones, mark exact centerline at 25-foot intervals.  *<br>__2) Maintain correct alignment with MOS centerline by checking distance between original centerline to every fifth 200-ft MOS centerline station (i.e., every 1,000 ft).<br>__3) See "Craters" procedure if damage is on the MOS. |
| Table 5.2. continued on next page. ||

| Procedure | Actions |
|---|---|
| __ 4. Edge Reference | __1) Establish left edge reference marks from threshold to station 400.<br>   __ a) At 400-ft point, place alignment cone on left edge of MOS.<br>   __ b) One person, at left corner threshold cone, sights along the two cones & directs cone placement at 200-ft point.<br>__2) Repeat process at opposite end.<br>__3) Consider placing right edge reference cones to allow completion of one end before moving to opposite end. * |
| __ 5. PAPI | __1) Locate inside PAPI unit by placing two stacked cones 950 feet from the threshold and 50 feet from left edge of the MOS.<br>__2) Adjust this PAPI distance as required based on variations in elevation and as necessary to avoid conflicts with other systems, obstacles, and pavement features.<br>__3) Site outside PAPI unit by placing a single cone 20 feet outboard of the two stacked cones. |
| __ 6. MAAS (AGM) | __1) Locate MAAS position based on coordinates provided by the SRC/DCC.<br>__2) Place a cone at both MOS edges at MAAS location.<br>__3) Place second cone 3 ft outboard of both edge cones. |
| __ 7. Craters | __1) Mark both sides of crater repairs with cones.<br>__2) Set up a T-zone/pattern at least 100 ft from the edge of both sides of crater. *<br>__3) Maintain 200-foot spacing of centerline cones through the crater repair area. * |
| __ 8. Taxiway Stripe(s) | __1) Taxiway entrance.  Place three traffic cones in a triangle at the entrance to a taxiway.  Place two cones on the edge of the MOS and the third cone is located where the taxiway centerline intersects the MOS.<br>__2) Stripe change-of-direction around existing damage.<br>   __ a) Place a mark at the start & end of each segment of the curve.<br>   __ b) In lieu of cones, use marking paint or Keel to mark exact location of each segment and at a minimum, the middle of the curve segment.<br>   __ c) If cones are used, determine required offset to left of  intended centerline with the Marking Crew. This distance will be based on the method of marking (i.e., Hand Wand or Paint Striper). * |

Table 5.2. continued on next page.

| Procedure | Actions |
|---|---|
| __ 9. Holding Position(s) | __1) Determine locations of taxiway holding position lines. Lines are normally sited 100 feet from edge of the MOS.  *<br>__2) Place two stacked cones on each end of runway holding lines.  Holding lines are parallel to MOS surface. |
| __ 10.  Approach Zone * | __1) Sighting along the centerline cones, place 7 cones outboard of the threshold at 200-foot separations.<br>__2) Move cones 2 feet to the right such that they align with the exact MOS centerline. |
| __ 11.  EALS Generator Location | __1) Identify location for generator/regulator based on selected MOS and Pre-Attack siting.<br>   __a)  Adjust siting based on damage to pre-sited area, MOS length, & a level area within 25 feet of the generator to allow placement of the fuel supply.<br>   __b)  Place a single cone 50 to 200 feet from the MOS near the midpoint of the MOS to identify the generator/regulator location.<br><br>   __c) Notify ADR Team Chief & EOD of location & access routes to add to safing & clearing efforts.<br>   __d)  Coordinate with EALS team on their installation timeframes and priorities. |
| __ 12. EALS priority: DTG Markers and AGM | __1) When the EALS must be deployed prior to placement of markers, check with EOD to ensure the areas along the side(s) of the MOS have been safed.<br>__2) At each AGM location, place a single cone on the right side of MOS (for unidirectional operation) or on both sides (for bidirectional operation).  See **Table 3.2.** regarding placement. |
| __ 13.  MOS Runway Immediate Launch | __1) Obtain the list of minimum markings and coordinates for the end points.<br>__2) Determine resources required to provide minimum marking required by SRC.<br>__3) Locate both ends of the MOS and layout the exact centerlines and corners with cones.<br>__4) Layout edge reference cones for first 400 feet on both sides of the MOS.<br>__5) Use visual alignment and tape measure(s) to layout any other specific minimum markings for the MOS. See **Table 5.3.** for specific marking steps as applicable. |

*Notes* **for Table 5.2.**

**Step 2.3):** When placing the exact centerline cones and threshold corner cones, use a bright marker (such as pavement spray paint or marking Keel) to mark locations. Mark a small "X" (about 6-inchs long) on pavement under the exact centerline cones before offsetting them. Mark under each threshold corner cone with a small "90° angle" mark (i.e., ↰, ↱, ⌊, and ⌐) that points toward the threshold centerline cone and along the MOS edge. This will ensure reference points can be quickly found and reestablished if the cones are knocked over during runway recovery efforts. Marking also helps the Paint Striping Crew confirm they are marking on the correct side of the marked centerline. Without a mark, this can be much harder to determine at night, in chemical gear, and with reduced visibility caused by smoke from bomb damaged facilities.

**Step 3.1):** If there is a pre-existing runway identification system, station marker posts may be used as a guide for laying out the 200-foot distances. If not available, establish a pattern to quickly measure the distances using the measuring tape and pacing steps. Pacing steps may not be possible if chemical gear is worn.

**Step 3.1) a):** See Pre-Attack **Table 5.1.**, Step 6.6) to adjust offsets.

**Step 3.1) b):** When using paint markings in lieu of cones, marking the pavement at 25-foot intervals is required to allow the Paint Striping Crew to maintain sighting alignment. Develop a marking technique to identify the 100-foot and 200-foot station points. One suggested method is to use 6-inch long letters such as the following:

> Intermediate 25-foot markers = "**X**"
>
> The 100-foot station markers = "**X/1**"
>
> The 200-foot station markers = "**X/2**"

The "X" provides an exact centerline location and the paint machine will obliterate most marks while painting. [See Pre-Attack **Table 5.1.**, Step 6.6) about adjusted offsets.] The marks can be seen from the edge of the MOS to aid in placing the markers at the 200-foot stations.

**Step 4.3):** If there are crater repairs within or along the MOS, edge obstructions may be present or there may be disruptions to normal marking procedures. When the MOS is longer than 7,500 feet, it may be difficult to use only left side alignment cones at opposite ends of the MOS. This is also the case when the MOS is partially obscured by smoke or darkness. Consider using right side alignment cones at the 200- and 400-foot stations in addition to the left side alignment cones.

**Steps 7.2) and 7.3):** The T-zone should be located at the closest 200-foot interval spacing marker that is at least 100 feet from the edge of the crater. See example of a typical layout in **Figure 5.1.** Avoid setting the T-zone within a large debris field that will not be cleared prior to painting. Maintain the 200-foot spacing through the area of repair.

**Figure 5.1. Typical T-Zone Layout at a Crater.**

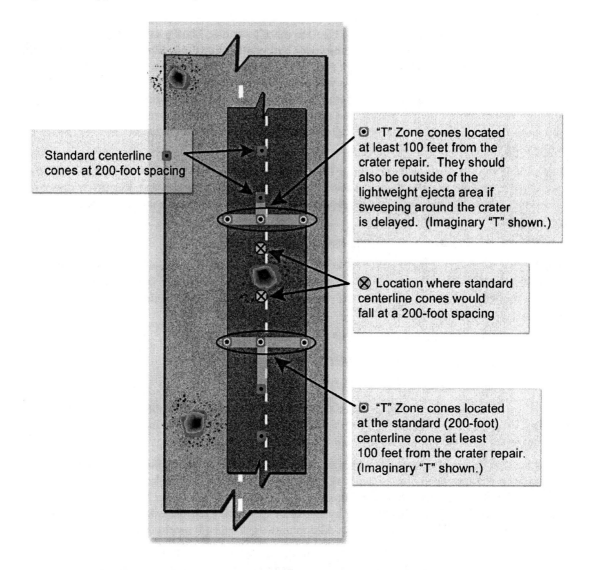

Standard centerline cones at 200-foot spacing

⊙ "T" Zone cones located at least 100 feet from the crater repair. They should also be outside of the lightweight ejecta area if sweeping around the crater is delayed. (Imaginary "T" shown.)

⊗ Location where standard centerline cones would fall at a 200-foot spacing

⊙ "T" Zone cones located at the standard (200-foot) centerline cone at least 100 feet from the crater repair. (Imaginary "T" shown.)

**Step 8.2) c):** The offset for painting will almost always be left of the required taxiway centerline stripe to prevent crossing over fresh centerline stripes, or other segments of the taxiway stripe. The Paint Striper is usually set up for the left gun of the gun carriage. The offset distance for painting the taxiway centerline stripe will depend on whether the Paint Striper or the Hand Wand is used. [Check with the Paint Striping Crew leader to determine the offsets required.] Normally, if the turns are tight or close together, the Hand Wand must be used. If in doubt about the offset distance, make a small centerline mark ($^C_L$) on the pavement using a bright marker to designate where the actual taxiway stripe is required. The Painting Crew will see the mark and adjust the offset as necessary.

**Step 9.1):** The MOS edge distance adjustment may be required under several circumstances; two examples follow.

If the taxiway is located at an acute angle of 45 degrees or less **and** cargo aircraft (i.e., the C-130 and/or C-17) will use the MOS, the taxiway holding line may have to be set back farther. Locate the taxiway holding line far enough back to prevent any portion of the wing from extending closer than 100 feet from the MOS edge. A distance of 125 feet from the MOS edge will prevent intrusion.

If the taxiway is located at an acute angle with the MOS **and** a large radius turn is required, the taxiway holding line may have to be set back farther than 100 feet from the edge of the MOS. Locate the holding line at least 10 feet outboard from where the end of the large radius curve intersects with the centerline of the MOS taxiway.

**Step 10:** EOD must assess and render the approach lighting zones safe before approach lighting cones are laid out. UXO clearing priorities will likely delay placing cones in the approach zone until MOS cones have been placed and markers are being laid out. Steps in **Table 5.2.** are based on laying out the approach zone near the end of the layout process.

5.3.2. The marking procedures in **Table 5.3.** are normally accomplished during the layout process. The procedures can vary based on the situation, such as when one end of the MOS has UXO safing and clearing operations underway, or the MOS has several craters under repair in an area with a great deal of debris. **Figure 5.2.** depicts a typical layout for the MAOSMS markers.

**Table 5.3.  Marking Crew Post-Attack Procedures: Placing Markers.**

| Procedure | Actions |
|---|---|
| __ 1.  Responding to Airfield | __1) Ensure that areas where markers are required have been assessed and safed by EOD.<br>__2) Ensure debris removal from the same areas.<br>__3) Make final determination of vehicle routes. |
| __ 2.  Threshold | __1) Deposit 10 edge marker bases & tops on each side of the threshold.<br>__2) Have one person place and assemble the threshold markers while the other crewmembers proceed.<br>__3) Place the base of the first marker away from the edge of the MOS at the predetermined setback distance.<br>__4) Set remaining 9 bases in a straight line out from the MOS with a 4- to 6-inch separation between each base.<br>__5) Attach the "V" tops to each base.<br>__6) Repeat on the other side of the MOS.<br>__7) Threshold installation member aligns markers, by sight, to the initial placement of edge markers by the other crewmembers, and then rejoins the crew after installing the 20 markers on one end.<br>__8) Repeat when you get to the other end of the MOS. |
| __ 3.  Edge Markers | __1) Proceed from threshold markers along one side of the MOS & offload one edge marker base & top opposite the 200-foot station cone/mark on the MOS centerline.<br>  __a) Do not place an edge marker at the two stations past a unidirectional MAAS.<br>  __b) Do not place an edge marker at the two stations before and after a bidirectional MAAS.<br>  __c) Check the MAAS run out configuration.  If configured for a 1,200-foot run out, remove a third edge marker if within approximately 550 feet of the MAAS when the MOS is narrow.<br>__2) Place base of markers away from MOS edge at predetermined setback distance.  Put in line with inside threshold marker between 4 & 10 ft from edge of MOS. |
| Table 5.3. continued on next page. ||

| Procedure | Actions |
|---|---|
|  | __3) Assemble each edge marker base by aligning the edges of the hook and loop fasteners on the tops and bases, and firmly pressing them together.<br><br>__4) Continue down the MOS edge to install markers at every 200-foot station.  The first two markers on the left can be installed by measuring off the left edge reference cones.  Align remaining edge markers by line of sight—the person installing the threshold markers can assist with alignment until rejoining the crew. |
| __ 4. DTG Markers | __1) Install DTG markers on right hand side of MOS, facing, and in descending order from, the operational threshold. If the MOS is bidirectional, DTG markers will also be a on Marking Crew's left side as it proceeds from operational threshold toward departure end of MOS.  Place left and right DTG markers directly across from each other at designated stations.  Ensure signs on left are placed facing, and in descending order from, the departure end opposite from those on right side of MOS.  *<br><br>__2) Locate & place first DTG marker as you come to the appropriate 200-foot station.*  The setback distance from the runway is normally 25 ft –see Emergency Criteria and Limitations in **Table 3.1.** regarding placement conflicts.<br><br>__3) Assemble and place the marker and sandbag anchoring (see **Attachment 2**).<br><br>__4) Install remaining DTG markers at subsequent 1,000-foot stations. |
| __ 5. MAAS (AGM) | __1) Locate and place the first AGM on the right side facing toward the primary operational threshold.<br><br>__2) For bidirectional MOS, place second AGM on left side of MOS facing in opposite direction of first marker.<br><br>__3) Normal setback distance from runway is 25 or 35 ft back from the runway edge, based on placement of DTG markers and MAAS.  See **Table 3.2.** Emergency Criteria and Limitations regarding placement if there are conflicts.<br><br>__4) If a second MAAS is deployed and used, repeat the above steps and try to place signs at the same setback distance, if possible. |

**\*Notes for Table 5.3.**

Step 4.1): Install DTG markers on right hand side of MOS. If the MOS is bidirectional, there will also be a DTG marker on the Marking Crew's left side as it proceeds from the operational threshold toward the departure end. Place left and right DTG markers directly across from each other at the designated stations. Ensure signs on the left face in the opposite direction from those on the right.

Step 4.2): When the MOS is an even increment of 1,000 feet (example: 4,000-, 5,000-, and 6,000-foot long), the DTG markers can be placed at 1,000-foot intervals. If the MOS is not an even increment of 1,000 feet, adjust the location of the DTG markers as described in **Table 5.4.** and illustrated in **Figure 5.3.**

**Table 5.4.  Adjusting DTG Marker Distances.**

| Adjusting Procedure | Example |
|---|---|
| Take the distance that is not a multiple of 1,000 and divide in half. | - A MOS is 6,600 ft long and is bidirectional.<br>- Divide the 600 ft by 2.  The result is 300 ft. |
| Add the result to the 1,000 feet at each end of the threshold. | - Add the result to 1,000 feet.<br>- The sum is 1,300 feet. |
| If this distance would fall between the 200-foot edge markers, then align the first DTG marker with the edge marker toward the threshold. | - The distance 1,300 feet from the operational threshold would fall between the 1,200- and 1,400-foot edge markers.<br>- Move right side DTG marker to the edge marker closest to the operational threshold.  This would be the 1,200-foot edge marker. |
| If the MOS is bi-directional, align last DTG (the number 1 DTG) with first DTG marker located nearest the threshold used most often (i.e., the primary operational threshold). | - Place a "**5**" DTG marker at this location on the right side of the MOS **facing toward** the primary operational threshold<br>- Place a "**1**" DTG marker directly opposite on the left side of the MOS **facing away from** the primary operational threshold<br>- Adjust distances such that the (primary) departure end receives the additional distance if DTG markers fall between edge markers |

**Figure 5.2.  Typical Placement of MAOSMS Markers.**

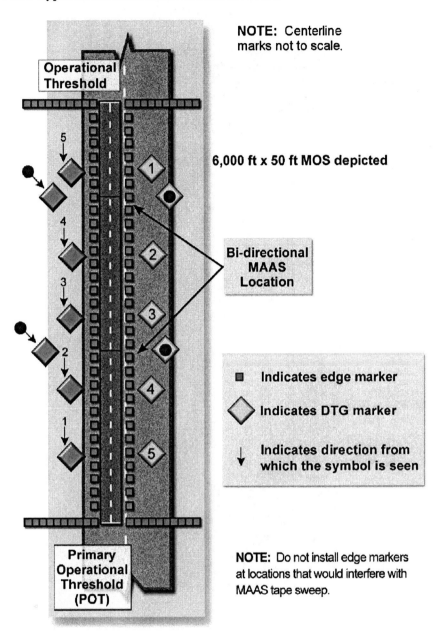

NOTE:  Centerline marks not to scale.

6,000 ft x 50 ft MOS depicted

Operational Threshold

Bi-directional MAAS Location

■  Indicates edge marker

◇  Indicates DTG marker

↓  Indicates direction from which the symbol is seen

Primary Operational Threshold (POT)

NOTE:  Do not install edge markers at locations that would interfere with MAAS tape sweep.

**Figure 5.3. Example for Adjusting DTG Marker Distances.**

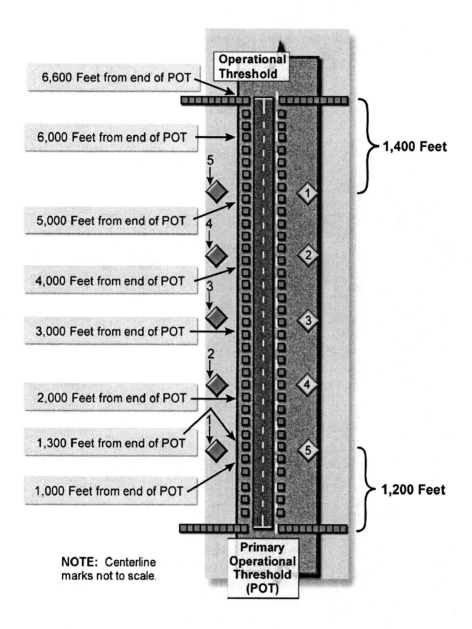

**5.4.  Post-Attack Procedures for the Paint Striping Crew.** Perform the procedures in **Table 5.5.** after an attack, or when establishing a bare base airfield with poor or no markings.

> **Warning**
> Do not place hands under an operating paint or bead gun. High pressure may inject paint or beads under skin and cause serious personal injury.

> **Caution**
> The Paint Striping set's guns, tanks, filters, & lines must be completely flushed & cleaned with water before & after each use to prevent clogging or erratic performance.

> **Caution**
> Beads must be kept dry to work properly.  After painting, all beads must be removed from bead tank, lines, and guns to prevent clogging.

**Table 5.5.  Paint Striping Crew Post-Attack Actions.**

| Procedure | Actions |
|---|---|
| __ 1. Vehicle/Equipment Checkout and Employment | __1) Ensure that vehicle and trailer are still operable. |
| | __2) Check installation of system components (i.e., tanks, guns, filters, and lines) and flush the systems. |
| | __3) Based on damage, repair and marking efforts, determine order of painting. |
| |    __a)  Coordinate with ADR Team Chief for a sweeper & grader to pass over centerline prior to striping. |
| |    __b) Normal procedure is to load and paint with: |
| |      __ (1)  White paint for the airfield markings, |
| |      __ (2)  Black paint to obliterate conflicting airfield markings, and |
| |      __ (3)  Yellow paint on the access taxiway(s) and holding positions. |
| |    __c)  Make a final determination on the amount of paint and beads that will be required (based on a travel speed of 3 MPH). |
| | __4) Agitate and load paint into the tanks.  * |
| | __5) Load beads into the tank. |
| | __6) If operating on the trailer, load solvent for flushing and an additional paint drum, if required. |
| __ 2.  MOS Striping with White Paint | __1) Threshold: |
| |    __a)  Paint the 30- to 36-inch wide operational threshold T-line using the traffic cones or pavement marks (if used in lieu of cones) as a guide.  The "T" line is the full width of the MOS. |
| |    __b)  It is best to start painting the centerline stripe first & come back to paint initial threshold T-line, this will avoid tracking paint on the MOS. |
| |    __c)  When finished painting centerline stripe, paint departure end (or opposite threshold) T-line. |
| | __2) Centerline: |
| |    __a)  Set up the paint striper to paint the 30- to 36-inch wide stripes on the true centerline.  Use the traffic cones as the left edge guide unless pavement centerline marks are used in lieu of cones. |
| Table 5.5. continued on next page. | |

| Procedure | Actions |
|---|---|
|  | __ (1)  Paint a stripe starting at the threshold T-line. The stripe must be at least 50 feet long. If the length of the MOS can be divided in even increments of 100 feet, then the initial and end stripe lengths at the Ts must be 75 feet in length (see **Figure 5.4.**). <br><br> __ (2)  When MOS length can not be divided in even increments of 100 feet, adjust the threshold "T" centerline lengths as follows: <br><br> (a)  If less than 50 feet remain after dividing MOS by 100 foot increments, make end stripes 75 feet long plus half the remaining length beyond 100 foot increments (See **Figure 5.5.**). <br><br> (b)  If precisely 50 feet remain after dividing MOS by 100 foot increments, T centerline lengths will be 50 feet long (See **Figure 5.6.**). <br><br> (c)  If more than 50 feet remain after dividing MOS by 100 foot increments, make end stripes 50 feet long plus half the remaining length beyond 100 foot increments (See **Figure 5.7.**). <br><br> __b)  When encountering a repair area, bypass area and continue marking centerline on other side of repair. Stripe repair area when time permits, but check with ADR Team Chief before going back. <br><br> __3)  Flush and clean out the Paint Striper system. <br><br> __a)  Load with paint and glass beads (if required) for the next painting operation. <br><br> __b)  Check to ensure that nozzle tips used next are properly adjusted, or changed if necessary. |
| __ 3. Obliteration | __1) Coordinate obliteration requirements and priorities with DCC for markings within, adjacent to, or near the MOS and MAOS taxiways.  * <br> __2) Black out runway markings that might cause confusion. **DO NOT USE GLASS BEADS.** |
| Table 5.5. continued on next page. ||

| Procedure | Actions |
|---|---|
|  | __3) When encountering a repair area, bypass the area and continue black out procedures on the other side of the repair.  Black out the repair area when/if time permits, but check with the ADR Team Chief before going back. |
|  | __4) Black out access taxiway markings for unusable taxiways and lines.  Also see *Unusable Access Taxiway Marking* below.<br><br>__a)  Lines that are within 50 feet of the MOS.<br><br>__b)  Existing taxiway marks within the first 50 feet of the unusable portion of the taxiway.<br><br>__c)  Begin blackout at a point where aircraft can change direction of taxi or stop and turn 180 degrees within the available taxiway width.  This point should be provided by the DCC.<br><br>__5) Flush and clean out the system.<br><br>__a)  Load with paint and glass beads (if required) for the next painting operation.<br><br>__b)  Ensure nozzle tips used for the next operation are properly adjusted or change if needed. |
| __ 4. Taxiway Lines | __1) Taxi Stripe Set-Up:<br><br>__a)  Set up guns on the Paint Striper and the Hand Wand to provide 6-inch wide stripes.<br><br>__b)  Determine the offset required for using the Paint Striper and/or the Hand Wand.<br><br>__c)  Reload Paint Striper with yellow paint & beads.<br><br>__d)  Layout of simple arcs.  If turn radius is a simple arc, use the tape to find start & stop point of arc.<br><br>__(1)  Hold one end of the tape at the center location of the arc.<br><br>__(2)  Turn the radius and place a cone or mark on the pavement at the start and end of the line and at three equally spaced points around the arc between the first two cones/marks.<br><br>__e)  Layout of a more complicated/longer radius arc.* |
| Table 5.5. continued on next page. ||

| Procedure | Actions |
|---|---|
| | __(1)  Mark pavement for taxiway lead-on & lead-out points for taxiway stripe.  At least 5 locations on arc are required to layout most arcs.  Use marker paint in lieu of cones if area is to be trafficked. |
| | __f) Layout of lead-on/-off straight sections, |
| | __(1)  Place a cone/mark every 50 feet for the 200-foot  distance for the nose-wheel guideline stripe on the MOS from the end of the arc. |
| | __(2)  Place a cone/mark at the taxiway centerline 5 feet from the taxiway holding position and a second cone/mark midpoint between the holding position cone/mark and the cone/mark at the end of the arc(s). |
| | __g)  For all cones, offset the cones the required amount to the left of the centerline of the actual paint striping mark.  [The Paint Striper should travel to the right of the reference marks and make right hand sweeping turns in order to stay off the fresh centerline paint.] |
| | __2) Painting Lead-in and Lead-out Nose-wheel Guidelines.  Paint according to the set up for reference cones or marks.  If marks were placed on the pavement in lieu of cones, set up Paint Striper or Hand Wand directly over the marks.  If cones were used, set up Paint Striper or Hand Wand based on required offsets. |
| | __a)  Paint a continuous 6-inch wide taxiway stripe. |
| | __b)  Stripe should run 200 ft parallel to MOS centerline with 3-ft offset on taxiway side of centerline. |
| | __c)  The taxiway turn is painted as an arc to intersect the taxiway centerline.  It becomes the taxiway centerline at the end of the arc. |
| | __(1)  Place a cone/mark at start of the nose-wheel guideline arc 3 feet from the MOS centerline.  If the MOS is bidirectional or the taxiway accesses the MOS in both directions, two arcs may be required for each taxiway. |
| | Table 5.5. continued on next page. |

| Procedure | Actions |
|---|---|
| | __(2)  Place a cone/mark at the termination location for the arc(s) where they meet the taxiway centerline or common intersecting point. |
| | __(3) Lay out middle section of arc(s) by placing 1 cone/mark in middle and 2 cones/marks midway between middle & end cones/marks. |
| | __d)  Paint the taxiway centerline to a point 5 feet short of the taxiway holding line. |
| | __e)  If there is a guideline on the other side of the taxiway centerline to another 3-foot offset at the MOS centerline, then set up at the point of tangency with the taxiway centerline and the first arc. |
| | __f)  Paint this stripe along the reference cones or marks to a point 200 feet down the MOS centerline from the termination of the arc. |
| | __g)  When using the Hand Wand in lieu of the Paint Striper, spread glass beads manually.  * |
| | __3) Holding Lines: |
| | __a)  Between the double-stacked cones designating the taxiway holding line, paint a solid 6-inch wide line 100 ft from and parallel to the MOS. |
| | __b)  6 inches from the MOS side of the solid line, paint a dashed line, alternating dashes & spaces every 3 ft. |
| | __4) Change in access taxiway direction curves are marked with the maximum radius possible.  Do not stripe straight stretches of taxiway. |
| | __5) Unusable Access Taxiway Marking: |
| | __a)  Paint a yellow "X" on the centerline of the blacked out portion of the taxiway marks.  Each leg of the "X" is 1 foot wide and 6 feet long. |
| | __b)  Paint the "X" 50 feet from the edge of the MOS. This distance may vary based on requirements for obliteration of unusable taxiways. |
| Table 5.5. continued on next page. | |

| Procedure | Actions |
|---|---|
| __ 5. Manual Painting | __1) If the Paint Striper fails, manual painting will be required.  Contact the ADR Team Chief to advise that manual painting will be required and to obtain manual painting priorities and requirements. |
| | __2) Obtain 2-gallon paint sprayers from ADR trailer. |
| | __3) Fill the paint sprayers with required paint color for striping and blackout. |
| | __4) Spray the MOS centerline at least 6-inches wide using the paint sprayers for takeoff operations. |
| | __5) Widen the line to the required (minimum of 30 inches) width for landing operations when time permits. |
| | __6) Use paint rollers to spread paint evenly.  Rollers can widen the lines, make them uniform, and to spread out the paint for faster drying. |
| | __7) If the paint striper is not working, then hand spread glass beads while painting.  * |

*Notes* for Table 5.5.

**Step 1.4):** If paint has previously been stored in the tank for short periods of time, scoop off any skin that may have formed on the top of the paint and then stir/agitate as required. Some paints can be stored up to 3 weeks in the paint tanks if a 1-inch layer of thinner is floated on top of the paint. Scoop out the thinner prior to using the paint.

**Step 3.1):** The blackout priorities vary based on the type of aircraft operations to be conducted, and the location of the MOS. Below are the normal areas that must be blacked out to prevent conflicts with MOS marking or prevent confusion and distraction for the pilots. **Table 5.6.** provides a prioritized list of obliteration priorities. **Figure 5.8.** provides an example of MOS obliteration requirements. Also, see **Attachment 3** for standard airfield marking nomenclature designations. When time is available during initial runway layout, blackout painting may be accomplished prior to other painting. If MOS markers and EALS components will be placed over or near areas to be obliterated, consider blacking out these areas earlier to avoid conflicts with placement of the markers and EALS components.

**Step 4.1) e):** Figure 5.9. shows the placement of cones or marks for the layout of typical taxiway lines. Also, follow Taxiway Paint Striping Layout procedures in the Basic Configuration Layout section.

**Steps 4.2) g) and 5.7):** One suggested expedient method to spread glass beads is to load the glass beads into sandbags. Numerous bags can be preloaded and stacked for use. Punch several small holes on one side at the end of the bag. The holes should be just large enough to allow the glass beads to flow from the bags when lightly shaken. Immediately after the paint has been hand sprayed and rolled out, shake the beads over the fresh paint. The paint should be of sufficient thickness after rolling to allow partial imbedding of the beads, but not completely covered. *Warning*: Any beads that do not adhere to the paint could pose foreign object damage (FOD) potential for aircraft engines and must be cleaned up before the airfield is opened for aircraft operations.

**Table 5.6.  Normal Blackout Priorities.**

| Markings on MOS | Markings in Approach Zone |
|---|---|
| 1. Threshold Marking | 1. Threshold Marking |
| 2. Designation Marking | 2. Designation Marking |
| 3. Centerline Marking | 3. Centerline Marking |
| 4. Aircraft Arresting System Markings (if out of service) | 4. Aircraft Arresting System Markings |
| 5. Unserviceable Taxiway Lead In/ Out Lines | 5.  Touchdown Zone Markings |
| 6. Touchdown Zone Markings | 6.  Fixed Distance Markings |
| 7. Fixed Distance Markings | |

**Figure 5.4.  MOS Centerline Striping Adjustment (When MOS is in even 100' increments).**

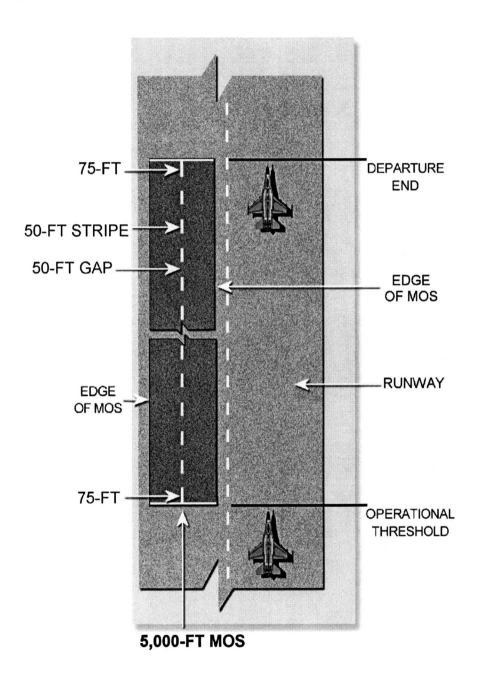

**Figure 5.5.  MOS Centerline Striping Adjustment (When less than 50-ft remains after dividing into 100-ft increments).**

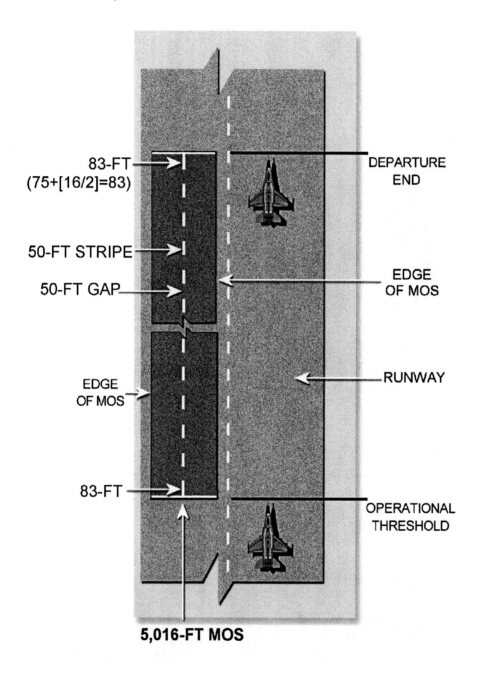

**Figure 5.6.  MOS Centerline Striping Adjustment**
**(When precisely 50-ft remains after dividing MOS in 100-ft increments).**

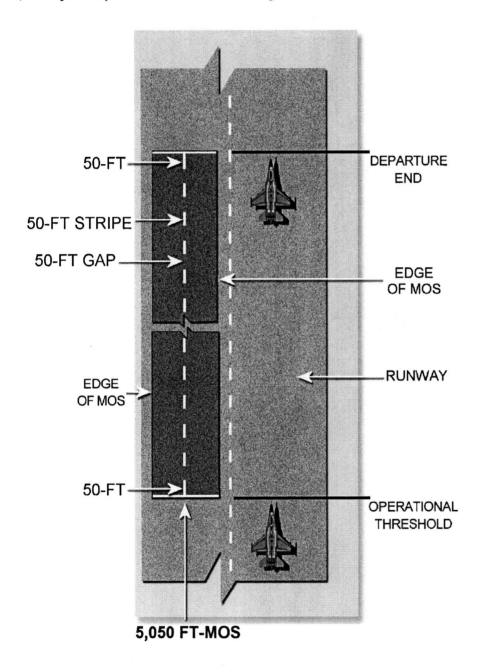

**5,050 FT-MOS**

**Figure 5.7.  MOS Centerline Striping Adjustment**
**(When more than 50-ft remains after dividing MOS in 100-ft increments)**

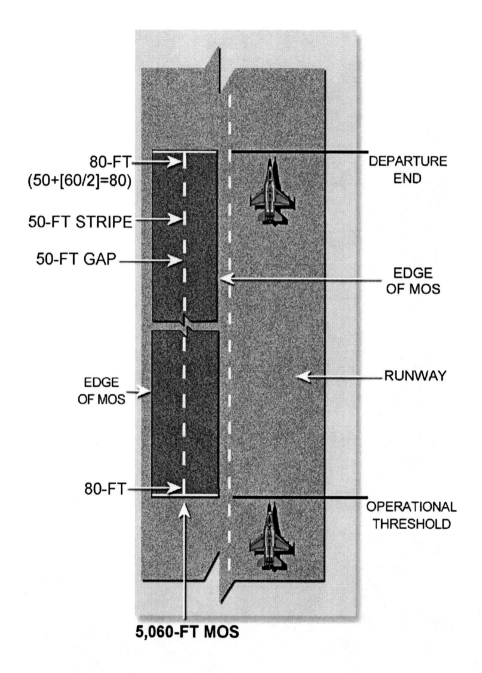

**Figure 5.8.   Example of MOS Obliteration Requirements.**

**Figure 5.9. Typical Direction-of-Travel for Taxiway Stripes**

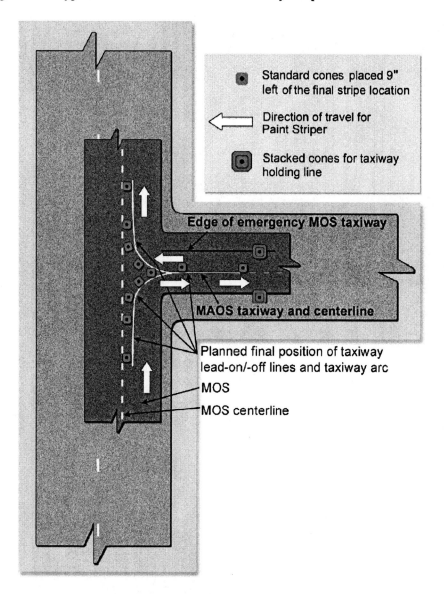

# Chapter 6

## SYSTEM RECOVERY

**6.1. Recovery Procedures.** Use procedures in **Table 6.1.** when the DCC directs removal of the installed MAOSMS. Usually the whole system will be recovered at one time unless the airfield is to be upgraded for further use.

**6.2. Contingency Airfield Equipment.** If the airfield will become a contingency airfield, some of the markers, the paint striping equipment, and the EALS will remain for further use. The DCC will direct the degree of recovery, or redeployment and use.

**Table 6.1. MAOSMS Recovery.**

| Procedure | Actions |
|---|---|
| __ 1. Edge Markers | __1) Obtain a large utility truck, or truck with a flatbed trailer, and drive along the edge of the MOS. |
| | __2) Separate edge marker tops from their bases and stack on utility trailer for transport to packaging area. |
| | __3) At packaging area, clean edge marker tops and bases with water and a cloth or a soft bristle brush, if necessary. |
| | __4) Dry tops/bases and repackage.  Ensure packaging includes an opaque cover for ultraviolet light protection. |
| __ 2. DTG markers and AGMs | __1) Obtain a pickup truck (or use same large utility truck or a truck with flatbed trailer to pick up edge markers). |
| | __2) Pick up the DTG markers, sandbags, and AGMs. |
| | __a) Reverse procedures of Attachment 2 to disassemble the upright stands |
| | __b) Reverse procedures of Attachment 1 to disassemble the sign faces. |
| | __c) Store sandbags for future MAOSMS use or use for hardening of base facilities. |
| | __3) Clean the flexible faces and all stand components with water and a cloth, or soft bristle brush. |
| | __4) Dry components and repackage markers. |
| Table 6.1. continued on next page. | |

| Procedure | Actions |
|---|---|
| __ 3. Paint Striping Set | __1) Bead tanks.<br><br>  __a) Remove all beads from the bead tanks.<br><br>    __(1) Scoop out the beads or<br><br>    __(2) Disconnect a bead gun hose & blow beads into a clean container with 10 to 15-PSI.<br><br>  __b) Give each air solenoid a light shot of lubricating oil or WD-40 in the exhaust port and the small hole above the port.<br><br>  __c) Release pressure from the bead tank.<br><br>__2) Paint tanks.<br><br>  __a) Empty the paint tanks using low pressure. If paint was temporarily stored in the tanks, ensure manual removal of any paint skins.<br><br>  __b) Remove paint tips; soak and clean with solvent.<br><br>  __c) Flush the paint tanks with compatible solvent using no more than 500-PSI.<br><br>  __d) Relieve the pressure in the system.<br><br>__3) Clean the high-pressure paint filters.<br><br>__4) Ensure that there is special pump lubricant (Lubrisolv) in the wet cup of the paint pump.<br><br>__5) Follow TO 36C35-7-1 to perform other required procedures for maintenance and preparing for storage.<br><br>__6) Wash entire paint striping set and store in a warm, dry place. |

DONALD J. WETEKAM,  Lt General, USAF
DCS/Installations & Logistics

**Attachment 1**

## GLOSSARY OF REFERENCES AND SUPPORTING INFORMATION

*References*

FAA Advisory Circular 150/5340-1H, *Standards for Airport Markings,* 8/31/1999

FAA Advisory Circular 150/5345-28E, *Precision Approach Path Indicator Systems (PAPI)*, 7/16/2004

AFPAM 10-219, Vol. 4, *Rapid Runway Repair Operations,* 1 Apr 1997

AFI 32-1042, *Standards for Marking Airfields*, 16 Mar 1994

AFMAN 32-1076, *Design Standards for Visual Air Navigation Facilities*, 1 Dec 1997, (soon to be UFC 3-535-01, *Airfield Lighting Systems*)

AFJPAM 32-8013, Vol. II, *Planning and Design of Roads, Airfields, and Heliports in the Theater of Operations—Airfield and Heliport Design*, 29 Sep 1994

AFI 33-360, Volume 1, *Air Force Content Management Program—Publications*, 30 January 2004

AFH 10-222, Volume 7, *Emergency Airfield Lighting System (EALS)*, 1 September 1999

TO 35E2-6-1, *Minimum Airfield Operating Surface Marking System MAOSMS), Layout and Marking Procedures with Illustrated Parts List for Rapid Runway Repair,* 5 Sep 1995

TO 35F5-3-17-1, *Operation and Maintenance Instructions—Lighting System, Airfield, Emergency A/E 82U-2 (Multi Electric Manufacturing, Inc.) 80302,* 1 Oct 2001

TO 36C35-7-1, *Operations and Maintenance Manual With Illustrated Parts Breakdown—Paint Stripping Set, Model AF120SET/AL120-EZ, Diesel Engine Serial MD/1-MD/2 (Duets) MD75-95, MD150-151, MD199-196, MW150-151-190, -191, MM150-1919-F15-F25 (EZ Liner Industries),* 13 Jul 1995

AFQTP 3E3X1-37.1.9, *Contingency Airfield Marking Paint Striper, DITIS # 777011708,* Mar 2003

*Abbreviations and Acronyms*

**ADR**—Airfield Damage Repair

**AGM**—Arresting Gear Marker

**C$_L$**—Centerline

**CE**—Civil Engineer(ing)

**DCC**—Damage Control Center

**DTG**—Distance to Go

**EALS**—Emergency Airfield Lighting System

**EOD**—Explosive Ordnance Disposal

**FAA**—Federal Aviation Administration

**IAW**—In Accordance With

**MAAS**—Mobile Aircraft Arresting System

**MAOS**—Minimum Airfield Operating Surface

**MAOSMS**—Minimum Airfield Operating Surface Marking System

**MOS**—Minimum Operating Strip

**MPH**—Miles Per Hour

**PAPI**—Precision Approach Path Indicator

**POT**—Primary Operational Threshold

**PRMS**—Pavement Reference Marking System

**PSI**—Pounds Per Square Inch

$R_m$—Minimum Taxi Turning Radius

**RRP**—Runway Reference Point

$R_{smooth}$—Smooth Curve

**SRC**—Survival Recovery Center

**TO**—Technical Order

**UXO**—Unexploded Explosive Ordnance

*Terms*

**Bi-directional Runway**—A runway that can support aircraft operations in both directions.

**T-Zone**—A "T" marking with traffic cones on either side of a crater that has not been repaired during layout of a MOS.

**Inboard/Outboard**—Describes the placement of an EALS component relative to the runway (or taxiway). View inboard as closer to, and outboard as farther from, the paved surface.

**Runway Edge**—One of the long sides of the runway/MOS. EDGE A is the side in the clockwise direction from end A. EDGE B is the other side.

**Runway End**—The longitudinal limit of usable runway opposite the runway threshold. It often, but not always, coincides with the threshold of the opposite direction runway surface. Red lights mark the runway end. The runway approach threshold/departure end is where an EALS team begins installing the system. END A threshold/end is where TEAM A begins. END B is the opposite threshold/end where TEAM B begins.

**Runway Threshold**—A line perpendicular to the runway centerline designating the beginning of that portion of a runway usable for landing. Green lights mark the threshold end. When the threshold of a runway is co-located with the end of the opposite runway, the threshold/end lights have a split lens with green on one side and red on the other.

**Unidirectional Runway**—A condition where, for whatever reason, aircraft takeoff and land on the runway in only one direction. If that condition is not temporary, approach lights and strobes are required only at the approach end, and place distance-to-go markers and lights only on the right side of the runway.

**Runway Designation**—A two-digit number that designates the magnetic heading of a runway. As viewed from an inbound aircraft, measure the heading of the runway centerline clockwise from magnetic north. Round the compass reading to the nearest 10 degrees, and drop the last digit (a zero). For example, when the magnetic heading of a runway/ MOS is 068°, the runway designation is 07 (round 068 to 070 and drop the last digit). When viewed from the opposite direction, consider the pavement a separate runway, and its designation is 25 (180° in the opposite direction). Painted designations are normally on ends of runways, but not on a MOS (see **Figure A4.4.**).

**Runway Reference Point (RRP)**—The RRP is the point on the runway centerline where the PAPI visual glide path intersects the runway.

**Approach Zone**—That end of the runway nearest to the direction from which the final approach is made. In relation to the EALS, the 1,400-foot clear zone before the MOS/runway threshold where approach zone lighting is installed.

**Obliteration**—To do away with previous airfield pavement markings by painting over them with black paint.

**Attachment 2**

**STANDARD PRE-ATTACK SIGN FOLDING INSTRUCTIONS**

**A2.1.** (Figure A2.1., Step 1)

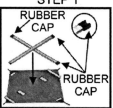

STEP 1

**Figure A2.1.**

A2.1.1.  Spread sign face down on a flat surface.

A2.1.2.  Position cross-brace perpendicular over sign face such that the cross-brace decal "TOP" faces up.

A2.1.3.  Ensure that the cross-brace tip without a rubber is positioned at the bottom corner of the sign face.

STEP 2

**A2.2.** (Figure A2.1., Step 2)

A2.2.1.  Fold the ½-inch straps over the tip of the vertical rod of the cross-brace.

A2.2.2.  Fasten the ½-inch bottom straps as shown.

**A2.3.** (Figure A2.1., Step 3)

A2.3.1.  Fasten the two interior straps and the top strap on the vertical rod.

STEP 3

**A2.4.** (Figure A2.1., Step 4)

A2.4.1.  Do not fasten side straps on horizontal rod.

A2.4.2.  Turn horizontal cross-brace to vertical position.

A2.4.3.  Roll the sign face up around the cross-brace.

A2.4.4.  Secure with the long strap.

STEP 4

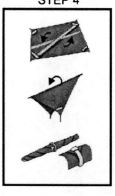

**Attachment 3**

**VERTICAL SIGN ASSEMBLY DIRECTIONS**

**A3.1.  (Figure A3.1.,** Step 1)

STEP 1

**Figure A3.1.**

A3.1.1.  Pull out the telescoping leg of each sign-holder until the detent button on the inner section of the leg automatically snaps into the matching hole on the outer section and locks into place in the fully extended position.

A3.1.2.  Ensure that legs are fully extended to prevent signs from tipping over under high wind.

STEP 2

**A3.2.**  (See **Figure A3.1.,** Step 2)

A3.2.1.  Drop all four legs one at a time by pulling on the locking pin to release the legs.

**A3.3.**  (See **Figure A3.1.,** Step 3)

A3.3.1.  Grasp the holder upright and lift stand about a foot to allow leg holders to fall into their locked position.

STEP 3

A3.3.2.  Ensure that the center of the holder is 2 to 3 inches above the ground.

**A3.4.**  (See **Figure A3.1.,** Step 4)

A3.4.1.  If the sign is on uneven ground, individually adjust and position the leg to another hole.

STEP 4

**A3.5.**  (See **Figure A3.2.**, Step 5)

**STEP 5**

**Figure A3.2.**

A3.5.1.  Sign legends are printed on the corners of the previously rolled up signs.

A3.5.2.  Select the sign face with the required legend and unroll the sign.

A3.5.3.  Turn cross-brace perpendicular to each other.

**A3.6.**  (See **Figure A3.2.**, Step 6)

A3.6.1.  Pull the sign's face taught and pull the ½-inch strap out and over the tip of the cross-brace.

A3.6.2.  Fasten the strap to the cross-brace strip.

A3.6.3.  Fasten the side straps together over the fastened strap.

**STEP 6**

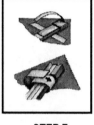

**A3.7.**  (See **Figure A3.2.**, Step 7)

A3.7.1.  Slide the bottom end of the vertical cross-brace into the channel upright on the stand.

**STEP 7**

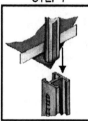

**A3.8.**  (See **Figure A3.3.**, Step 8)

STEP 8

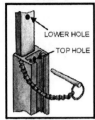

**Figure A3.3.**

A3.8.1.  Slide the vertical brace into the upright channel until the top hole of the channel aligns with the lower hole of the cross-brace.

A3.8.2.  Lock the sign face into the sign base by inserting the hitch pin through the two holes.

A3.8.3.  Ensure that the hitch pin is completely through both holes.

**A3.9.**  (See **Figure A3.3.**, Step 9)

A3.9.1.  Fasten the sign side straps around the upright channel of the base.

STEP 9

**Attachment 4**

**SUPPORTING GRAPHICS FOR RUNWAY/MOS RELATED TERMS**

**Figure A4.1.  Terms Related to Unidirectional MOS.**

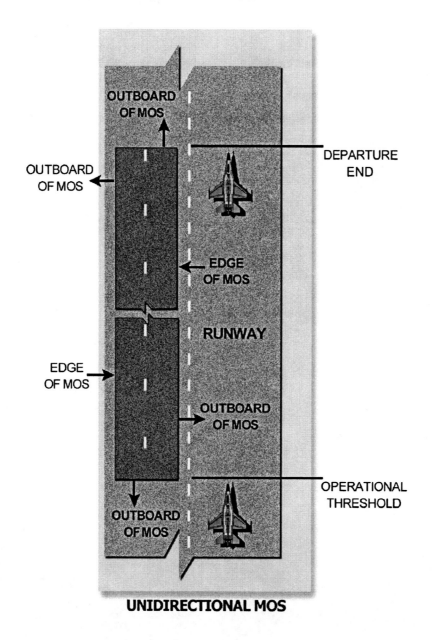

**Figure A4.2.  Terms Related to Bidirectional MOS.**

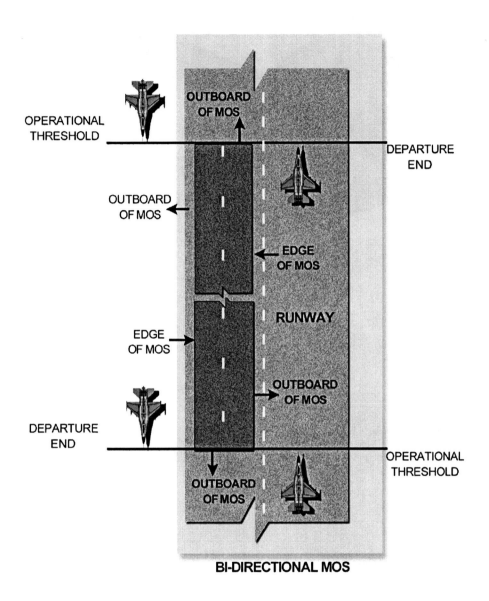

**BI-DIRECTIONAL MOS**

**Figure A4.3.  Runway Orientation.**

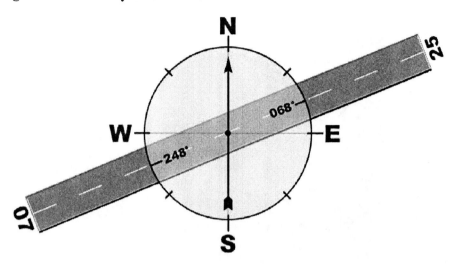

**Figure A4.4.** depicts basic marking configuration for jet runways longer than 4K-ft; relates to categories listed in **Table 5.6.** for obliteration priorities. Contingency locations may vary from standards.

**Figure A4.4.  Standard Airfield Marking Nomenclature.**

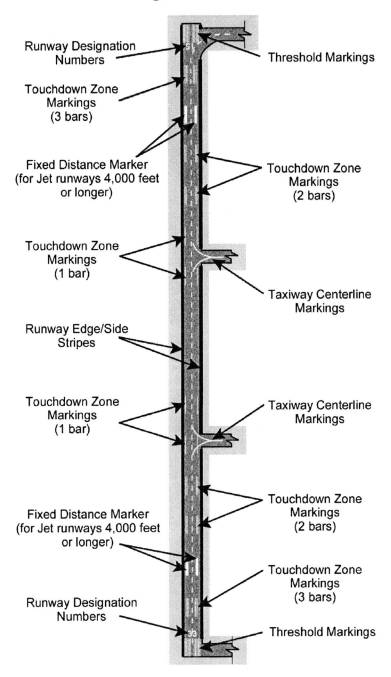

CPSIA information can be obtained at www.ICGtesting.com
Printed in the USA
BVOW06s0441010415

394083BV00032B/231/P